Howard Finster
The Early Years

A private portrait of America's premier folk artist

MW00603807

Howard Finster
The Early Years

A private portrait of
America's premier
folk artist

Thelma Finster
Bradshaw

CRANE HILL
PUBLISHERS

Copyright © 2001 by Thelma Finster Bradshaw

Book design by Tim Kolankiewicz

All original woodburned frames by Howard Finster, from the Thomas E. Scanlin collection

Items in the Thomas E. Scanlin collection photographed by Tim Kolankiewicz

All rights reserved. With the exception of brief quotations in critical reviews or articles, no part of this work may be reproduced or transmitted in any form or by any means, electronic or mechanical, including photocopying, recording, or any information storage and retrieval system, without permission in writing from the publisher.

Published by Crane Hill Publishers
www.cranehill.com

Note: Every effort has been made to trace the copyright holders of photographs used in this book. Crane Hill Publishers apologizes for any unintentional omissions and would be pleased, in such cases, to add an acknowledgment in future editions.

Printed in Canada

Library of Congress Cataloging-in-Publication Data
Bradshaw, Thelma Finster.
   Howard Finster : the early years : a private portrait of America's premier folk artist /
Thelma Finster Bradshaw.
       p. cm.
    ISBN 1-57587-171-8
    1. Finster, Howard, 1916- 2. Folk artists--United States--Biography. 3. Outsider
art--United States. 4. Bradshaw, Thelma Finster. I. Title.

N6537.F464 B73 2001
709'.2--dc 21
[B]

                                                                                    2001042391

10   9   8   7   6   5   4   3   2   1

CONTENTS

THE STRANGE HOWARD FINSTER
YOU ARE THE LIGHT THAT BRIGHTENS MY NIGHT.
AND SET THE STARS IN MY SKYE.
TO SURCH THE WORLD. THERES NON LIKE YOU
UNTIL THE DAY i DIE.
YOUR PEACE IS CALM. AS THE MORNING SUN.
ON THE FLOWER OF THE SPARKLING DEW
i WILL SEARCH NO MORE TO FIND A FRIEND
THAT WILL CLASS UP WITH YOU.
YOU HEARD ME WHEN i CALLED. AND LISTENED
TO WHAT i SAID SO i MADE UP YOUR FEATHER
PILLOW AND LAID iT UNDER YOUR HEAD.
i PRAY YOU WILL LIVE IN WEALTH AND FAME.
KEEP GOD AT YOUR RIGHT HAND. HE WILL TAKE
YOU THROUGH THE WINDING ROADS.

IMPASSABLE TO ANY MAN. WHEN YOU ARE OLD AND
FEEBLE HE WILL BE STANDING BY TO WIPE AWAY
EVER TEAR
WHEN YOU HAFTO
CRY.
MY GIFT IS ON
PAGE 169 THE
GOD GIVEN TALENT
i LEAVE BEHIND
MY STORY IS ON
PAGE 172.
April 19. 1979.
Howard Finster

ACKNOWLEDGMENTS

Without the efforts and interest of others,
the task of writing *Amazing America*
would have been considerably more difficult.
In acknowledgment, we want to establish
THE JANE AND MICHAEL STERN HALL OF FAME.

Charter Members:

KATHY MATTHEWS—For singular editorial acumen,
an inspiration and a joy to work with.

DAVID OBST—For his enthusiasm,
which served as a foundation for our energies.

BETTY ANNE CLARKE—For careful guidance and good advice.

Howard Finster wrote this poem on April 19, 1979, to his daughter, Thelma. He was featured in the book, Amazing America, *and wrote the poem in the front of her copy of the book.*

THE STRANGE HOWARD FINSTER

You are the light that brightens my night
and set the stars in my skye.

To surch the world, there's non like you
until the day I die.

Your peace is calm as the morning sun
on the flower of the sparkling dew
i will search no more to find a friend
that will class up with you.

You heard me when i called and listened
to what i said so i made up your feather
pillow and laid it under your head.

i pray you will live in wealth and fame.
Keep God at your right hand. He will take
you through the winding roads
impassable to any man.

When you are old and
feeble he will be standing by to wipe away
ever tear
when you hafto cry.

INTRODUCTION

Long before the world knew Howard Finster as an artist, he was my father.

I am grateful that during the past several years, others have finally recognized what I've always known about the man who raised me. Howard Finster is a humble, unselfish man whose primary mission in life has always been bringing people to God.

If you gaze at one of his paintings long enough, you'll realize he's not painting for himself. He paints for each and every one of you.

If you're not personally acquainted with God, my father hopes his paintings will introduce you to Him. With his art, he tries to show each

of you a little piece of Heaven that could be yours if you'd only let God walk into those empty spaces in your heart.

Roy Gene and I pose with Dad around 1955, just before going to church. Behind us is the wall of my father's workshop, where he repaired bicycles and did woodwork. I'm about ten years old here; Roy Gene is about fifteen.

My father is a rare man. Despite the fame and fortune that have come his way in recent years, he doesn't truly claim the honors or the accolades. He knows God has fed him those visions all his life and that God finally gave him the courage to paint them. Since my youth, since he began painting, the only thing that has changed about my dad is how he preaches. A Baptist preacher by trade, he now uses paint instead of the pulpit to deliver his sermons.

There are times I wish I could take my dad back to the

Howard at his easel in Paradise Garden, 1987.

time when I was growing up—to all those peaceful years before I had to share him with everyone else. But such a wish is selfish. He has too much to say to the world, too many souls to save, and too little time to deliver all the messages that weigh so heavily on his heart.

I consider it a blessing that I had all those years with him before he became famous. Now I want to share some of those memories with all the people who only know my father as an artist. There is much more to know about him than all those paintings hanging on art gallery walls. His art is wonderful; but, more important, he also is a wonderful father.

I am fortunate to hold the memories that I do from my childhood. My mother and father never had much money, but they provided my brother, my sisters, and me with a wealth of childhood memories that can't be priced. I can never hope to thank my parents enough for all they've given me. And for all those memories, for all the ways my parents have shown their love for me throughout the years, I dedicate this book to them. I dedicate this book to my father, who always taught me right from wrong, and to my mother, who kept me walking down a straight path with all her bedtime prayers and keen hickory switches.

Now I say to the people of this world: Howard Finster belongs to you.

I hope you listen to what he has to say. And I sincerely hope you cherish the moment if you ever have the opportunity to meet him. He calls me his guardian angel, but my father is the one who has wings.

Thelma Finster Bradshaw

Thelma Finster Bradshaw

CHAPTER 1
Walking in Heaven Among My Father's Mansions

My father didn't become famous until around the mid-1970s. Dad was in his late fifties when the world finally realized what I have always known as his daughter—that Howard Finster is a visionary with a mission to preach through his paintbrush. What most people don't know is that some of his visions of Heaven, of "mansions," and of other worlds had their start in our Trion, Georgia, backyard.

When I was growing up in Trion, we didn't have much money. We didn't go to ball games or the movies. Out of her own patterns, my mother made some of our clothes, including underwear from twenty-five-cent flour sacks. In high school, I remember getting twenty-six cents a day for lunch money. Our shoes were always well worn before we got a new pair. But I never felt poor, and I suspect my sisters and brother didn't either.

Dressed in their church clothes, my father and my sister Gladys pose behind a replica of Trion Baptist Church in 1955.

Our parents, with their ingenuity, made us rich. My mother sewed beautiful taffeta gowns for my sisters and me and hardy shirts for my brother. Our father built us "mansions" in our backyard, inspired by his visions of Heaven. They are no longer standing, but they still live in his paintings and in my memory. And the gowns and dresses my mother made for my dolls and me still make me feel rich when I think about them.

I'm convinced that during those years in Trion, my father was trying to build us Eden out of plywood, homemade tools, hard work, and an imagination fed by the hand of God.

Throughout our backyard, he built us the mansions he'd first dreamed about as a boy in Valley Head, Alabama. In his youth, he never had time to build those structures he imagined when he thought of Heaven. He and his brothers and sisters had to pick cotton and tend to an eight-acre farm to help keep food on

11

Mother and I pose in the doorway of our gazebo around 1950–52. In the foreground is a little frame house surrounded by chicken wire, where our chickens laid their eggs. My dad made a number of these houses to give our animals shelter.

Left to right: Roy Gene, Earline, Gladys, and I stand near a replica of Trion Baptist Church in our backyard. To Roy Gene's left is the entrance to our museum building. The tall building behind the church is a bird cage my father created.

the family table. But somehow he kept those visions alive in his mind all those years, and when he became our father, he was finally able to build the mansions he'd dreamed about as a boy. That's how we grew up—playing in my dad's vision of Heaven.

Dad painted our mansions white with green trim. There was the miniature replica of Trion Baptist Church, with its steeple and a real bell you could ring at dinnertime. We had a fourteen-foot castle, complete with little windows and doors, which towered above all the other buildings in our backyard. Scattered among the flower beds and walkways were all the little houses where our cats played, jumping through the doors and windows. Even our chickens had their own mansion where they laid their eggs and raised their young. After a time, my father had built so many mansions in our backyard that I lost count of them.

We had other special buildings and unusual attractions in our backyard. During long, lazy summer afternoons, we enjoyed the comfort of shade under the gazebo Dad trimmed with elaborate latticework. My parents dug a well from which cold, fresh drinking water flowed in a seemingly endless supply. Near our well and pump house we had an outdoor faucet. The water that ran from the faucet would trickle down to turn a water wheel Dad made from an old bicycle rim with little tin trays attached. You could always hear the sound of running water.

He also built a swimming pool that drew all the neighborhood children to our backyard. When we grew older, my father turned the pool into a pond where ducks swam in the place of children. And we were the only family I knew of who had the privilege of enjoying flowers year-round. From thick plywood, Dad built brightly painted six-foot flowers to brighten our yard. In front of one of our buildings stood a tall cross built out of cement he mixed himself. For me, the cross was a silent testimony to his lifelong mission to save people from sin.

Even the pathways in our backyard were made special. My father, who has always loved glitter and shiny things, built the walkways in our backyard with broken mirrors, brick, and cement. When the sun hit them just right, they glittered like bright jewels— just like the pathways he imagined winding through Heaven.

With all of the trees, budding flowers, and fruit, our yard truly resembled

Roy Gene and Gladys smile in front of the Trion Baptist Church replica. Our father's mansions made our yard a wonderful place to grow up.

Gladys stands next to our duck pond. My father originally built it as a swimming pool, but it was eventually converted into a home for some of our feathered friends.

what I picture when I think of Eden. Our little corner of paradise left me with many pleasant memories that have sustained me all these years. In early morning hours throughout my childhood, Dad and I walked together down the glittering, winding paths in our backyard, picking raspberries and eating them right off the branch. He has always had a green thumb, and it seemed that he was forever planting flowers, working in the garden, or toiling away on some project to beautify our yard. We had beehives, rose bushes that sweetened the air, berries my mother made into jam, grapes we ate straight from the vine, and a big garden where we grew the tomatoes, potatoes, beans, carrots, and

My parents and I gather in front of our garden in Trion, where we grew corn, beans, okra, potatoes, and squash. All over the yard, my dad planted roses, grapes, and raspberries.

okra that ended up on our dining room table. Sometimes, as a special treat, we were surprised with fresh honey and sweet, chewy honeycomb.

During those morning walks, Dad sometimes preached to me, teaching me lessons about life that I've carried with me since. One time, he preached about a vision he had—a prediction that a famine one day would sweep across the land. He told me that when I grew up I should plant a big garden with plenty of fruit trees so I'd always have food to eat during hard times. I've since followed this advice. I believe both the vision and advice had something to do with his having gone to bed hungry during the Depression. During those lean years, my dad, his parents, and his brothers and sisters survived by eating black-eyed peas for almost every meal. I think that experience drove my dad to make sure we had plenty of food on our dinner plates. Although we were poor by most standards, my brother, sisters, and I never went to bed hungry.

I loved our garden, the raspberries, the shining sidewalks, and everything about that backyard in Trion. But there was one magical spot that fed my childhood imagination

This gold-colored dress was one of my favorites. My mother made it from flour sacks. On this day in 1955 I stand in front of the playhouse Dad built, holding my Bible and pocketbook, ready to go to church.

more than any other: the "mansion" my father made into our playhouse. He wanted us to feel as though it was truly a house of our own, so he installed real glass in the windows. At the entrance was a front porch where we could sit and watch the goings-on in our busy backyard. The roof of our playhouse was even fancier than the one on the house where we grew up. At the top was an octagonal dome with small windows on each side. My dad, who always seemed to attend to every detail, placed beautiful China dolls in all the windows of the dome. From every direction in our yard you could see one of those dolls staring back at you. The inside of our playhouse was special, too. We had a living room, a bedroom, and a kitchen, all furnished with tables and chairs my father had fashioned out of plywood. In the bedroom there was a foot-long bed built for our dolls to sleep in. My mother, intent on making the place even more of a home, added her own special touches with curtains she had sewn for us on her machine.

15

Our playhouse was situated right next to the house we grew up in—I suppose that was so my parents could keep an eye on us while we played.

I considered Olin more of a brother than a brother-in-law, because he married Earline when I was only ten years old. You can see some of my dolls peering out the windows in the playhouse dome.

Lost in my imagination, a world of dolls, and private tea parties, I never noticed my parents watching me. I spent many summer afternoons in that little house, playing mother to my dolls and cooking in my kitchen. My cooking was always best when our garden reached its summer prime. I would sneak vegetables out of the garden and "cook" fancy meals on an old grill I placed on a box in the kitchen of our playhouse. On Sundays after church, all my friends would come over, and I'd conjure up fancy main courses and mud pies on my "stove." In the nearby gazebo, which doubled as a pretend restaurant, I'd imagine I was a waitress and serve my friends dinner and mud pies decorated with flowers for dessert.

This doll bed, made by my father, resembles the one in our playhouse in Trion.

That playhouse was wonderful for a child's imagination. I spent hours playing inside our little mansion. I believe it was that playhouse, as well as the swimming pool my dad built, that drew children from all over the neighborhood. We never wanted for company.

It may seem hard to believe, but it never occurred to me until I was much older that all of our mansions set us apart from other children in town. I just always assumed every child had his or her own backyard park full of mansions, playhouses, and animals.

When I grew older, I also realized that we were the only kids for miles around who had a museum in our backyard. My father called it the Myers Museum, named after the people who originally owned the old building. The museum was rather plain before my father started working his magic on it. By the time he finished, the museum had been transformed. He wanted to add interest to the roof, so he built a spire that resembled the top of our backyard mansions. On either side of the spire, he placed wooden fans shaped in half-circles. He painted windows on the museum and hung dried sunflowers nearby. Near the bottom of the museum front, he built a wooden bird, a wagon wheel, and a wooden flower for added decoration.

The inside was just as unusual as the outside. Fond of old things and a collector at heart, my father filled the museum with antique guns, old coins, milk churns, a gramophone, harnesses, and old clocks people donated to him. Looking back on it, I think he must have been trying to collect every invention known to man in the space of that

My brother, in front of a cement cross my father made, obviously loved to clown around. Behind him is the museum, both sides of which were hung with sunflowers. We raised pigeons, which always gathered in the top of our museum.

building. I think that, as an inventor himself, my father wanted people to see the hand of God in ordinary, everyday things. And I suspect that's why he started that museum.

Roy Gene, a young teenager here, flexes his muscles in front of the museum building. He made his own weights by pouring cement into cans and attaching them to a metal rod. In front of him is another one of my father's mansions.

The collection really started growing after he began preaching at Chelsea Baptist Church in 1950. Members of the congregation added to it by donating antiques and castaway possessions. To show his appreciation, my father always placed the name of the donor on each item, along with the date of the gift. Some of his collection also came from items people had tossed away. As a young girl, I spent a lot of time walking through my father's museum, admiring all of his treasures.

With all these attractions in our backyard, it really should have been no surprise when the museum and all my father's mansions started drawing the attention and curiosity of our neighbors and other people all over our little northwest Georgia town. Attracted by the unusual, people began touring our backyard park. My father never charged admission to our backyard or the museum, but he set up a donation box that people filled with two or three dollars at a time. Even though we were poor, my father never kept the money. Throughout his life, he has made it his mission to help the disadvantaged, the downtrodden, and the disabled. And so when our donation box was full, my father

Roy Gene in front of the tall wooden fence that surrounded our yard in Trion. My father kept a donation box handy for sightseers. About once a month, he emptied the box and sent the money to a nearby home for disabled children.

sent the money to the Crippled Children's Home in Hapeville, Georgia.

Eventually, though, the museum had to be shut down because people started breaking into the building and stealing items. I still have the clock he gave me from that collection. I guess he wanted me to have something that would remind me of that exhibit house and the collection he spent so many years trying to build.

Even after he closed the museum, though, the greatest treasures of all remained in the attic. While I was growing up, my father raised pigeons in cages he built throughout our backyard. When they were old enough, he set the birds free, and they'd make

Roy Gene and Gladys in the backyard park. Behind Gladys are beehives that lined the edge of our property. My mother jarred the honey and gave us the honeycomb to chew. We found it better than store-bought candy.

their home in the attic of the museum. One time, as a late-night treat my father walked me up the tall ladder to the attic. With our flashlights we peered in at all the cooing birds busily raising their young. That trip to the top of the museum is one of my best memories.

I suppose most people would think it unusual to have the equivalent of a miniature city in the backyard and people constantly milling around. And I suspect not many people would think it normal to have the equivalent of a zoo in their backyard either. But during our years in Trion, living among our mansions, we had chickens, pigeons, cats, dogs, ducks, an owl, rabbits, a raccoon, a snake, and a goat named Nanny. We were never without animals, because it seemed someone was always dropping them off at our house. I suppose people knew we would readily adopt and care for these animals like so many orphans. Our backyard was a busy, crowded place.

My mother used to lament that we didn't have a normal yard like everyone else had. She worried that all the mansions crowded us children, leaving little room for us to run and play. But we had an open field nearby if we felt the urge to run, swings to play on, and a whole miniature city sprawling across our backyard that soon became the envy of children all over town. Our backyard was like a giant amusement park, and we never ran out of things to do or explore.

I couldn't have asked for a better playground— or a father with a greater imagination.

Even though my mother voiced occasional objections about our backyard, she was usually tolerant of my father's imagination, unusual projects, and artistic impulses. But the year he painted green polka dots in a checkerboard pattern all over our house she put her foot down.

Soon after my mother objected to the polka dots, my father busied himself by painting our cement-block house white again. This may sound

The building that contained our house and grocery store in Trion was built with my father's handmade cement blocks. At one point, he painted polka dots on the outside of our house, but Mother eventually persuaded him to paint it white again.

strange, but I didn't think growing up in a polka dot house was anything out of the ordinary. Whatever my father did always seemed to me the very thing that needed to be done. The artistic impulses he followed always had my unquestioning support and admiration.

Despite my mother's dislike for the green polka dots outside, she did give my father the freedom to experiment inside. In his mind, there's never been such a thing as building a room—or anything, for that matter—and leaving

My father stands in the doorway into our living room in Trion. This threshold was a testament to my dad's love of unusual and interesting details. He decorated the stained plywood door frame with oblong, oval mirrors and built trim along the tops of the walls down the hallway.

father's passion and talent for painting. He decorated the doorway to our living room with small oval mirrors. Around other door frames and through the hallways in our house, he placed elaborately carved trim that he designed and made in his workshop.

Of the many things I loved about that house, the hardwood floor in our living room was one of my favorites. When the floor needed buffing, I'd sit on a blanket or quilt, and Roy Gene would pull me back and forth across the floor until it shined again.

it unadorned or simply painted white. On the top half of one of our doors was a scene with cows, trees, and a pasture. Looking back on it, that painting was probably the first indication of my

My least favorite part was the flat roof, which sprang leaks during heavy downpours. Never one to let anything go to waste, my dad had gone around to service stations collecting empty oil cans, which he used with tar to shingle our roof. But his choice of oil cans for roofing material resulted in a near-constant repair job and an ever-dwindling supply of tar. My father spent a lot of time on that roof.

On the first floor below where we lived was the grocery store my parents ran to help keep food on our table. Between customers, my mother sat in back of the store, sewing our clothes, upholstering furniture, or refinishing wood furniture. My parents occasionally allowed us to pick out candy from the store, but my brother and sisters and I soon figured out we'd be able to get more candy if we helped ourselves when

Dad was a very busy man, but he always found time for his children. No matter how often we wrestled with him, we were never able to hold him down. This picture of Roy Gene, Gladys, Dad, and me probably was taken after a "wrestling match."

they weren't watching. It's a wonder my parents made any profit from their small business, because we'd sneak into the store when they weren't around and snack on candy, ice cream, hot dogs, and bologna. We never did figure out whether our parents caught on to our furtive shopping trips. But even if they had their suspicions, they left us alone to snack our way through the darkened shelves and coolers.

I do believe, though, that if we were ever caught in the act we would have been given a long sermon about the sins of stealing. Our father was always good at delivering his sermons.

23

CHAPTER 2
MIRACLES MADE IN
A WORKSHOP

Thomas E. Scanlin Collection

When Dad wasn't preaching, fixing up his "mansions," or busying himself around our yard, I usually found him tinkering in his workshop, where he was always juggling and laboring away on multiple projects. When I wasn't puttering in my playhouse, mothering my dolls, or playing with our cats, I was usually at my father's side for hours on end, watching him saw, hammer, and sand his woodwork.

I was always happiest when I was with my father in his workshop or anywhere he happened to be working, creating, building, or painting something. As a young girl, I quickly learned that if I was going to have any time alone with my father, I would have to tag along while he worked on his projects. He never sat around in his free time. It seemed the only time I could find him in one place

My father sits dressed for church in the doorway of our gazebo. One day when he was building it I climbed on the roof with him, resisting my mother's urgings to come down. If my father was building something, I had to be right there. To this day, I'm the only one out of five children who uses a saw and a sander.

for long was while he sat either at the dinner table or at his workbench. And so, I learned how to become a good shadow. Wherever my father walked with his toolbox, I was usually close behind.

Most times my mother didn't have a problem letting me out of her sight as long as I was with Dad. But shadowing him sometimes involved an element of danger, because his work often required him to climb and descend tall ladders. I remember one afternoon in particular when my mother discovered me high above the ground on the roof of our gazebo. I was only about five or six years old at the time, and Dad was putting the finishing touches on the roof. When my mother walked out of the house to call us in for lunch, she spotted me by his side, sitting next to him several feet above the ground. I remember her scolding my father and trying to coax me down from that roof, but I felt safe up there with him and refused to budge. In the end, and to my mother's dismay, my father let me stay on that roof with him.

Mom always tried her best to interest me in activities outside my father's domain. But cooking and sewing just didn't hold the same attraction for me as learning how to hammer nails into wood, refinish furniture, or rebuild a lawnmower. Thus, I didn't learn how to cook until after I was married. And even though my mother managed to teach me how to sew at a young age, I rarely set foot near her sewing machine unless she was trying to size me for a dress. I guess I was something of a tomboy. And while my sisters were practicing their piano, learning how to cook, and how to sew dresses, I could be found in my father's workshop, learning how to hold a hammer and saw wood. To me, the workshop was a truly magical place. It was a place where he always seemed to build something out of nothing. It

Thomas E. Scanlin Collection

Howard's first metal tools, turned on a lathe, were displayed like this in our first exhibit house.

was where he made his dreams and visions come true from a few used nails, a hammer, and pieces of wood he usually salvaged from old buildings or from people who wanted to get rid of their scraps. When I was growing up, it always seemed to me that my father was most content when he was in his workshop. He simply enjoyed the art of creating—whether it was a house, a "mansion," a kitchen cabinet, or a doll-sized set of living room furniture.

Most amazing to me is that Howard Finster never had any formal training or schooling on how to build something from wood, nails, and a hammer. Much of what he learned about carpentry and woodworking came from trial and error and from his father, Samuel William Finster. My grandfather was a sawmiller, and I suppose he must have passed on his love for invention and woodworking to my father.

My grandfather started teaching his son at an early age. When my father was just a young boy, he and his father salvaged an old motor

26

from a cotton gin and built a turning lathe together. With that machine—which my father kept and used for years—he and my grandfather shaped furniture legs, built wood trim, and designed many other pieces of furniture. When my father was sixteen years old, they used that turning lathe to build a full-size bed out of old walnut fenceposts from trees they had cut down from their property in Valley Head. This became the bed my parents slept in when they were married three years later, in 1935. I now have this bed.

Around the time they made that bed, my father built his first workshop, a log cabin on his parents' property. There was no money to go out and buy nails, so my grandfather cut his own out of heavy wire. Using those handmade nails, my father hammered together his workshop, where he spent hours building his first projects. He started out by making small wooden jugs and bottles with the turning lathe. Those early projects laid the groundwork for

Thomas E. Scanlin Collection

My father made this table around 1954. It stood in a corner of our living room, usually covered with a small round lace centerpiece made by family friend Beulah Garner.

all the mansions he built in our backyard in Trion, and they inspired many of the wood projects he later made and sold for profit when I was a teenager.

It was through collaborating on all those projects with my grandfather that my dad learned how to make do with what he had, as well as how to reuse and rebuild almost anything. I suppose growing up in a family that had little money taught my father the necessity of invention, resourcefulness, and creativity.

While I was growing up, our family continued to struggle financially. We sometimes lacked the money for new tools or machinery. But the lack of money never stopped my father from building anything. He built the foundation for our house out of cement and creek gravel, one square block at a time. And he was forever finding new uses for old things. Some of his woodworking machines were powered by old motors that he had rebuilt—just like the turning lathe he and his father had built together many years before. Sometimes my dad even made some

Dad made many cabinets for people. This one was for a woman in Lyerly, Georgia, to house her large doll collection. When I was a little girl, I daydreamed about owning a doll collection just like that of Mrs. Joe Cook.

of his own tools and wrenches. If a tool didn't exist for a job he needed done, he'd invent his own.

Long before recycling became a household word and the environmentally correct thing to do, my father made it a daily practice in his workshop. He built many of his projects out of old lumber, used tin, and old nails. If he had a piece of old lumber that still had nails in it, he would pull them out, straighten them, and reuse them for a new project. If something needed painting, he'd simply use the paint he had on hand, often regardless of the color.

Once I was old enough, I guess my father figured he'd put me to work—especially since I was always hanging around his shop anyway. He never forced me to work, but if I was looking for something to do and wanted to earn a little extra money, he'd find something I could do to help him out. Through practice and observation, I quickly became an old hand at pulling used nails from lumber and straightening them out. For every twelve nails I pulled and wriggled straight again, Dad would pay me a nickel.

Over time I was given the opportunity to help with many other projects, as my father's workload increased. People around town learned that he could do, build, or paint just about anything. He soon had enough work to keep him busy for months on end. Most of what he learned he taught himself. He built screen doors, made cabinets, painted signs for churches and businesses, painted houses, did plumbing and electrical work, repaired bicycles, refinished furniture, and even tuned pianos. Judging from the amount of work Dad did, I don't think he ever turned anyone or any job away. Even when he didn't know how to do a particular job, he'd still agree to do it anyway. My father has always had a lot of faith, and he always knew that with God's help he could figure out anything if he set his mind to it.

Out of all his undertakings, though, there was one Dad enjoyed more than any other: rebuilding and repairing bicycles. Most of his businesses were built on the idea of helping others, which certainly was the case with the bicycle business. My father firmly believed that every child ought to have a bicycle. But he also knew many children couldn't afford such a luxury. So my dad began rescuing old bicycles, old spokes, used-up gears, tattered seats, and well-worn handlebars. Most bikes he bought for one or two dollars apiece. With his large collection of tools, he took the old bikes apart, rebuilt them, refitted them with new tires, and dressed them up with a brand-new coat of paint. The bikes sold for ten to fifteen dollars apiece. Before long, it seemed as though almost every kid in town was riding around on one of my father's bicycles. This was no small feat, because in those days bicycles weren't as easily available as they are today.

I spent hours learning the finer points of rebuilding old bikes. I would have done the work

My father and my sister Beverly sit on the steps in front of our house, admiring the bicycles he has fixed up.

regardless of whether I was paid because it meant more time with my father. But he has always been a fair man, and I was paid for my hard work. One of my primary jobs in the bike business involved pulling spokes out of bicycle wheels and then straightening them with a tool my father created especially for that task. For each spoke I pulled out and straightened, I received a penny. A penny per spoke may not sound like much money, but I straightened a lot of spokes as a young girl. I

29

earned what seemed like a small fortune back then. I pitched in on other jobs, too. I painted so many bicycle frames that I eventually lost count. For each frame I rejuvenated with my paintbrush, I earned $2.50. I also spent a lot of time painting rusted tire rims with aluminum paint. While I was busy pulling out crooked spokes and painting bicycle frames, my father was rebuilding bike parts, attaching new seats, and affixing new pedals. Together we made quite a team—we were about as industrious as an assembly line full of workers. And by the time we rolled a bike out the door of the workshop, it looked and rode like new.

One day, after hours of hard work in the shop, my father surprised me with my very own bike—the best payment he ever gave me. Like the others that rolled out of my father's shop, my bicycle was

This is the bicycle my father made for me out of used parts. When we lived in Trion, he started building bikes from used parts and selling them for ten to fifteen dollars apiece—a price children in town could afford.

fashioned out of used gears, spokes, and handlebars. To this day I have that bike, and anytime I want to recapture part of my youth, I'll roll it out of our garage and ride it down the street in front of our house. It's painted a pretty light blue and is easy to spot from afar, with its banana-shaped seat and funny-looking handlebars. A few years ago, my father decided he wanted to make my bike even more special by doing art all over it. Unfortunately, as he grew busier and more feeble, it never happened. But he did sign the back fender, and I am happy with that. Even though it is only a twenty-inch bicycle, I rode it for years. After my children were born, I'd set them on the front part of the long seat, wrap one arm around them, and pedal my way all around the neighborhood. My younger boys, Paul and Eli, get embarrassed now when I ride my funny-looking bike in front of our house. But that bike still pedals like a dream, and when I get going fast enough and feel the breeze hitting my face, I once again become that little girl in a ponytail riding her bike for the first time through the streets of Trion.

My father gave me many other gifts from his workshop. He taught me how to take an old piece of furniture and make it look new again. He taught me how to paint signs with a steady hand. He also taught me how to fix a carburetor. But more important, my father taught me the right way to approach work. He taught me that if you put your mind to it, you can learn how to do just about anything. And he taught me that with a little hard work and a lot of ingenuity, you can transform any old

Thomas E. Scanlin Collection

A pair of dollhouse chairs my father made in the early 1950s.

thing used into something new and usable again.

During those early years in Trion, my dad built, repaired, and rejuvenated everything from doll furniture to motorcycles. And even though he was always busy working on one project or another, I suspect he never felt like he was working at all. He's always enjoyed working with his hands, finding new ways around problems that stood in his way, and creating beautiful things out of what others mistakenly considered trash. Then, and later after we moved to Pennville in the fall of 1961, my father's workshop was his haven, his own private sanctuary. Watching him work all these years, I always suspected that God was my father's third hand, his primary inspiration, and his best business partner.

Thomas E. Scanlin Collection

31

CHAPTER 3
A Visionary Is Born in
Valley Head, Alabama

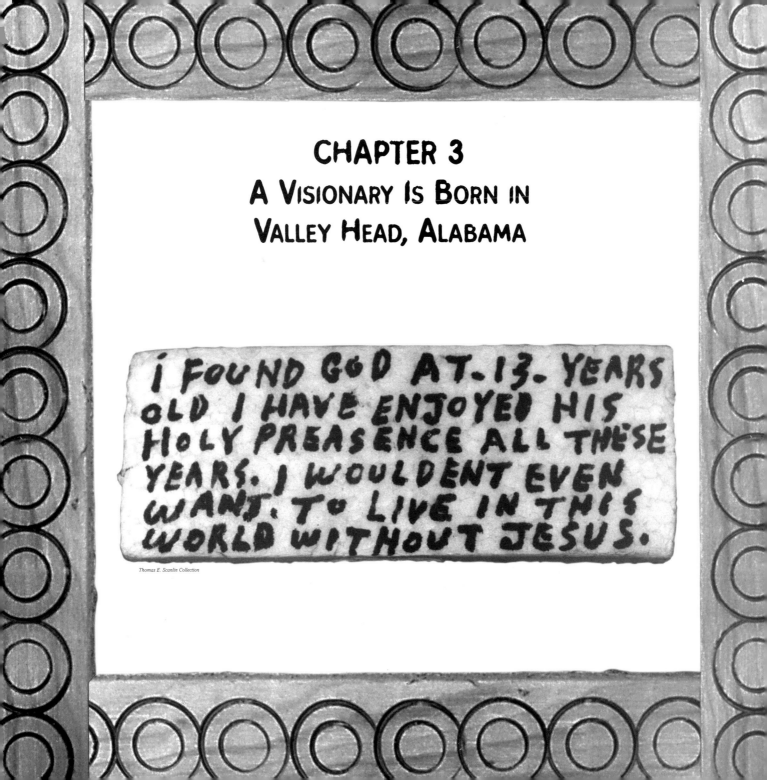

i FOUND GOD AT.13. YEARS
OLD I HAVE ENJOYED HIS
HOLY PREASENCE ALL THESE
YEARS. I WOULDENT EVEN
WANT. TO LIVE IN THIS
WORLD WITHOUT JESUS.

Thomas E. Scanlin Collection

My father has always been a religious man, and he's spent most of his life trying to save souls and bring people closer to God. I have always firmly believed that God handpicked my father on the day he was born to spread His word.

Howard Finster was born on December 2, 1916, the same year President Woodrow Wilson was elected to his second term in office. It was one year before the United States entered World War I. He grew up in Valley Head, Alabama, a small rural community in DeKalb County in the northeast corner of the state. The area where my father grew up is at the tail end of the Appalachian mountain chain, rich in scenery with tall mountains, lush vegetation, and deep canyons. But despite those beautiful vistas and landscapes, the region was populated at that time by poor, hard-working people trying to make their living off the land. The Finster family numbered among those people, and the life into which my father was born was full of hardship and heartache.

During his first years, my father lived in a two-story colonial house that sat on about forty-two acres of farmland near Lookout Mountain. My grandfather, Samuel, must have known he was destined to have a large family because he built that house with a lot of room. It had two porches, three or four bedrooms, a loft, a spacious kitchen, and a roof made out of shingles my grandfather had split by hand. Around the

This house was constructed from used wood that had come from the sawmill where Howard's father worked in Valley Head, Alabama. Pictured from left to right are brother Arthur, Howard in mother Lula's arms, sisters Betty and Lila, father Samuel, brother Fred, sisters Bernice and Abbie, and brothers Jack and Ora (on the porch).

Thomas E. Scanlin Collection

house he built a picket fence. My grandmother, Lula, accented the fence by planting brightly colored flowers. From the way my father describes it, that house must have looked stately to the people driving past on US 11. In fact, I'd be willing to bet none of the passersby would have guessed that my

Grandfather earned his living as a sawmiller and farmer. Occasionally he perfomed odd jobs for neighbors to make a little extra money on the side. One of those projects still stands today. It is a natural fence he built for a local doctor, made out of rocks he hauled from the mountainside. But even

grandparents and their thirteen children struggled every day to ward off poverty. They did not have the comforts we take for granted today. They had no electricity and relied on candles after nightfall. They didn't have running

Thomas F. Scanlin Collection

with farming, sawmilling, and all of the odd jobs, my grandfather and grandmother needed as much help as they could get to maintain their farm and bring money into the household. So as soon as the children were old

My father and his family in Valley Head, Alabama, where he grew up. His mother Lula and father Samuel lean against the car. In the middle from left to right are my father and his brothers Jack and Fred. Seated in the front from left to right are his sisters Bernice, Tillie, Betty, and Sue.

water or an indoor bathroom. And between the cracks in the floor they could see the chickens that were running around underneath the house.

With such a large family, keeping food on the table was a daily struggle for my grandparents.

enough, they were put to work on the eight-acre farm and the large cotton field.

My dad was no different from the rest of the children. Before the age of twelve he was picking cotton and plowing fields in the sweltering Alabama heat, along with his parents, brothers, and sisters. There was so much work to be done on the farm that my father was unable to go to school past the sixth grade. That's why he sometimes spells words a little differently from the way most people spell them. He has never said whether he regrets not being able to finish school, but my dad has more than made up for a lack of schooling with his curiosity, love of learning, and talent for teaching himself new things. Back when my father was growing up, it wasn't unusual for a child not to finish school. Families who made their living from farming usually needed more hands helping than the number they had at their disposal. Daily survival often meant twelve-hour days with little respite—work from sunup to sundown. Reading, writing, and arithmetic were considered luxuries that many families couldn't afford. Even though the schooling was free, time spent at school meant precious time away from the fields, and one less pair of hands to plow the fields and pick the corn.

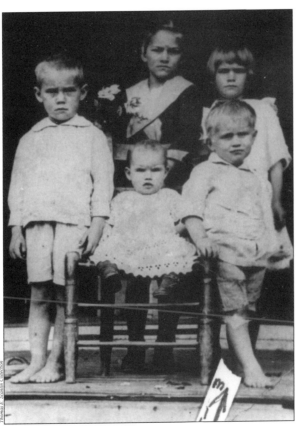

Howard, at age three, stands to the right of the chair in 1918. Also pictured (clockwise from right) are sister Sue in the chair, brother Fred, and sisters Bessie and Lila.

Farm life back when my father was growing up was a grueling existence. They didn't have fancy machinery or pesticides. My father and his family had to cut down their cornstalks and pick worms off their tobacco plants by hand. They had to gather their cotton by hand, too, and there were worms in the cotton that stung my father's fingers. Work started early in the morning and continued until dusk so that the family could sell their cotton to a local gin. It was backbreaking work, and, even at a young age, Howard Finster was already trying to figure out how to make life a little easier.

The blistering heat in the cotton fields was a constant problem. I suppose my father was trying to figure out how to make the long day's work a little

Howard's grandfather, Mose Henegar, holding the Bible, stands in front of the original log house in Valley Head, Alabama, in the 1890s. Grandmother Clara stands with him behind the table.

cooler when he decided to wear a dress out into the cotton fields one day. After all, the dress seemed as though it would be much cooler than overalls. But it brought on so much laughter and teasing from his brothers and sisters, my father never wore that dress again. After he started painting much later in life, he thought fondly of that afternoon and painted a picture of himself in that dress out in the middle of the cotton field. I suppose he wished to recapture the humorous moment. The Finster family did have its moments of laughter and light-heartedness, such as that afternoon in the cotton field. But those

moments were bitterly interspersed with a string of family tragedies.

When my father was just a young boy, his family's house burned to the ground. They lost everything they owned. Living out in the country with no fire department and a supply of water that couldn't match the tall, leaping flames, the family was forced to stand outside and watch their two-story house burn to the ground. For a time after the fire, they had to live in the building where they stored their cotton. Eventually, with the help of neighbors, my grandfather was able to rebuild on the same site, and that house still stands today. Even so, my dad never got over that day when he had to stand out in the yard, helplessly watching flames devour the house where he had spent the first years of his life. Throughout my childhood I remember he was always afraid of losing everything again. Every time we went away—even for a short time—he made us walk through the house and unplug every last appliance before we locked the doors and backed out of our driveway.

That house fire was but one calamity that struck my father's family. In those days, many children didn't live to adulthood. Medicine wasn't as advanced as it is today, and out in the country, hospitals and doctors were often miles away. My father remained healthy enough to survive those early years, but six of his brothers and sisters weren't as fortunate. Two of his brothers, Edgar and Johnie, died when they were only about four days old. One of the eldest brothers, Arthur, died from appendicitis when he was about sixteen. Gracie, one of the younger girls, died from pneumonia when she was seven. And Ora, one of my father's older brothers, died at age thirty-one after getting too close to a brush fire. Severely burned, Ora couldn't pull through and died two days later in the hospital.

The deaths of those siblings were hard on my dad. But the death of his older sister Abbie on April 5, 1919, probably has had the most lasting impact on him. Abbie helped take care of my father when he was growing up, and I suppose she was somewhat of a mother figure to him. One afternoon, when Abbie was thirteen years old, a trusted dog on the family farm went haywire and bit her, my grandmother, and my grandfather. After finding out the dog had rabies, they took a long train ride to a hospital in Birmingham, Alabama, where doctors injected a round of twenty-one shots

Thomas E. Scanlin Collection

A vision of his sister Abbie (left), seen here in 1912, is what would give Howard Finster his first religious experience. Sister Bernice is at right.

into each of their abdomens. Fortunately, my grandparents survived. But Abbie only lived a few short weeks after her return from the hospital. An incurable infection developed at the site of her shots, and I guess there wasn't anything the doctors could have done to save her. When she passed away, my father was too young to understand anything about dying. He didn't understand why his sister wouldn't come home and kept asking after her.

It was shortly after Abbie's death that my father had his first religious experience—his first glimpse of Heaven and the world beyond. He was only two or three years old at the time. One afternoon, he was standing in a tomato patch near the farmhouse, crying out for his mother, who was working in the fields. In between his tears, my father recalls looking up in the sky. There among the clouds was his sister Abbie. Wearing a long white flowing gown, Abbie began descending a staircase that seemed to unfold from the heavens. Startled to see his sister walking so high above the ground, my father began calling after her. But Abbie seemed unable to hear him and then began ascending the staircase. As she climbed her long white gown came open at her feet, exposing clothing that my dad recognized as hers. Abbie finally looked briefly over her shoulder at my father, and then disappeared from his sight forever. She evaporated into the clouds as suddenly as she had appeared. My dad told his mother about seeing his sister Abbie. Of course, my grandmother told him that he couldn't have seen Abbie—that she wouldn't be coming home anymore. At the time, having lost several children already, my grandmother feared her son's vision was a bad omen, a sign that he would be the next child to go to the Lord. Fortunately, her fears proved to

Howard painted this picture of his birthplace in 1976.

be unfounded in the literal sense.

My father's life changed that afternoon in the tomato patch. He still remembers that first vision, when God briefly allowed him a last glimpse of his sister. God has spoken to him through many visions since. It was a few short years later—partly because of that vision—my father realized his mission in life. Howard Finster knew in his heart that the Lord was calling him to preach His word.

He didn't tell his parents about his calling for a long time. Perhaps he was afraid they wouldn't believe him. The Finster family was not particularly religious, and they did not regularly attend church. But my great-grandfather, Mose Henegar, had made his living as a traveling preacher. And even though he died before my father was born, Mose Henegar must have passed on his preaching genes, because my father didn't get much religion at home.

In the heart of Southern Baptist country, going to church several times a week is as much a part of life as breathing. It's where souls are saved in daylong tent revivals during loud, urgent sermons about Revelations, the end days, and Hell fires. It's where preachers baptize the old-fashioned way, the same way John the Baptist baptized Jesus in the River Jordan. In God's country, where churches sit on almost every corner, religion easily seeped into my father's veins. And even though his parents didn't sit in a church pew several times a week, my father got plenty of religion sitting in the one-room schoolhouse that was used for church services on the weekends.

There was a special teacher who heavily influenced my father's spiritual development while he attended Violet Hill School. The teacher's name was Richard Phillips. Back then it wasn't frowned upon when talk of religion entered the classroom. Because of that, my father got a good dose of the Bible and the word of God at school every day. Richard was a God-fearing man who believed the best way to start out the school day was with the Lord's Prayer, a devotional, and the hymn, "When the Roll Is Called up Yonder." Richard taught my dad a lot about the Bible and nurtured the spiritual seed that had started to take root. So when my father was just thirteen years old, he was saved at a church revival near Violet Hill School. Bud White was the preacher at that revival, and he must have had some awe-inspiring message that day because my father was saved in the span of a few hours and felt the spirit of the Holy Ghost wash over him. From that day forward, my father made God the center of his life. Shortly afterward, Bud White baptized my father in a nearby stream.

After he was saved, my father began walking about a few miles to church every Sunday. Sometimes my grandfather would walk to church with him, but he always waited outside. On one of those Sundays, my father entered Lee's Chapel Church and spotted his teacher, Richard Phillips, sitting up in the choir. My dad sat down beside Richard and after several moments whispered into his ear that he felt called to preach. I'm not sure that my father expected

My father at sixteen (the age when he started preaching) and his childhood friend J. B. White. The two were schoolmates at Violet Hill School.

Richard to act on this confession so quickly. But moments later, Richard stood in front of the congregation and announced that Howard Finster had a message for the people. I imagine my father was pretty stunned, but he made his way to the pulpit and began preaching about how people have the choice between two paths in life: the path that leads to Heaven and the path that leads to Hell. He was only sixteen when he delivered that first sermon, and he's been preaching in one form or another ever since.

A few short years later, Howard Finster—through his ministry and patient persistence—saved his first soul. Even though my grandfather had walked him to church all those years, Samuel never would actually cross the threshold and enter the sanctuary with his son. After my father was saved, he began praying on his father's behalf and trying to talk to him about God. But for years my grandfather Samuel closed his ears to any talk of religion. Then one day, while the two men worked together in the yard, my father started praying in front of my grandfather. My dad says that after he finished praying his father seemed touched by the

Seated are my mother's parents, Noah and Mary Freeman. My mother, Pauline, at about age three, is in her mother's lap; my Uncle Floyd sits in his father's lap.

word of God. My father has always been very earnest when he prays, and it's no surprise to me that he was able to convert his father that way. Samuel died a few years later on April 30, 1936, but he died a saved man. Saving him was a great relief to my father.

By this time, church had become the center of my dad's life. It was where he started preaching his first sermons. It was where he first met God. And it was where he met my mother.

One Sunday, while my father was preaching at Sulphur Springs Baptist Church, a young woman stood up before the congregation and began singing. Her name was Pauline Freeman. She was a tall, slender blond with a beautiful voice. Howard Finster found her hard to forget.

About a year later, Pauline and her family moved from Sulphur Springs to Valley Head, not far from my father's house. This didn't escape my father's notice, and he appeared at their doorstep one afternoon to invite Pauline's mother to church.

The following Sunday, my father walked to church with Pauline and her mother. My parents began their courtship on their weekly walks to Sunday services. They'd sit on the porch swing at her house after church and talk. One thing led to another, and they had their first kiss after one of those walks home from church. Not long after that, my father asked Pauline Freeman to be his wife.

Fortunately, my father had won over Pauline's mother with his charm, because her daughter was just shy of eighteen, the legal marrying age. Pauline's parents had to sign a legal consent form for her to walk down the aisle. Much to my father's relief, her parents signed their consent, and my mother and father began planning for their wedding. With little money, though, there wasn't much planning to do. My father couldn't afford to buy a wedding ring at that time, but he did the best he could and surprised her with a wedding dress he had bought for $2.98. The color of the dress he picked out probably was one of the first indications that my mother was marrying a man who walked on the unconventional side of life. The dress he chose was a light turquoise, his favorite color.

My parents married in 1935—not in a church as you might expect, but in a cotton gin. The man who ran the cotton gin, Preacher "Doc" White, was the same man who bought all the cotton from my grandfather's farm. And apparently, Preacher White had such a thriving operation that if you wanted him to preside over your wedding ceremony you had to tie the knot at his place of business, surrounded by all those bales of cotton.

After the ceremony, my father and mother moved into an old, shacklike building behind his parents' house. Howard was the only one of the Finster children still living on the farm at that time; he had remained behind to help his parents keep up with all the work in the cotton fields and their garden. When he wasn't working in the fields, my father was traveling around the countryside, preaching the word of God. Despite all of his work, though, there was little money for furniture or other household items during the first few years of my parents' marriage. Their pay on the farm was what they pulled out of the garden for dinner. And even though my dad was regularly traveling and preaching, many of the country churches were nearly as poor as my father. Often, the highest pay a congregation could afford was their gratitude and vegetables picked from their own gardens. Unlike most newly married couples today, my parents didn't return home from their wedding with a new set of dishes, silverware, or furniture. At first, their only furnishings consisted of a bed my dad and his father had made and an old wood-burning stove. Even with so few worldly possessions, though, my parents recall that they were very happy during those first years of marriage. They had each other, they had God, they had food and a roof over their heads, and I guess they figured that was all it took to be happy.

My parents lived on the farm in that one-room house for about two years, until the late 1930s. During that time, my grandfather passed away, and my grandmother's health took a turn for the worse. No longer able to care for herself, my grandmother decided to move to Trion, Georgia, to live with Betty, one of my father's older sisters. For a while, my parents stayed behind in a valiant effort to keep the family farm running, but maintaining all those acres of farmland was too much work for two people. Plus, by then they were raising their first child, my oldest sister Earline. It eventually became too difficult for my parents to make ends meet on the farm in Valley Head. So, like my grandmother and my father's sister Betty, my parents packed up their few belongings and moved just over the state line to Trion.

Lookout Mountain was a favorite destination for my family. In this photograph, my parents pose arm in arm on the mountain in the 1940s.

CHAPTER 4
Traveling and Saving Souls in the Bible Belt

1944

200 CONVERTS SAVED IN MEETING 1944

Thomas E. Scanlin Collection

HEAR

Floyd Crowe, Pastor Pennville Gospel Tabernacle, and Howard Finister, Pastor Rock Bridge Baptist Church, in an Old-Fashioned

TENT REVIVAL

HERE IN FORT PAYNE

Tent Located on Gault Ave., Near Davis Hosiery Mill

AUGUST 28 THROUGH SEPTEMBER 9

SERVICES EACH EVENING 8:00

Everyone Welcome 1944

The small town of Trion, Georgia, has always revolved around the textile industry. At the time my parents moved there, Riegel's Cotton Mill was the company where most people earned their living, inspecting cloth and denim. I guess you could say Trion, like many other southern towns, was basically built by the mill. People who lived in town usually lived in one of the small, neatly kept houses built by the company. When residents shopped in Trion, they usually went to a mill-built store called the Big Friendly, a large department store that sold everything from clothing to hardware. Anyone in Trion who didn't work at the mill either farmed or raised cattle for a living, but those residents were few and far between.

I guess my dad felt he'd had enough of farming by the time he moved to Trion. So after renting a house from Betty, he, like most everyone else in town, applied for a job at the mill.

My parents stand in front of Aunt Betty's house in Trion, Georgia, before I was born. This was shortly after they moved from the farm in Valley Head, Alabama.

During the first few months at the cotton mill, he had to ride his bike to work. In the winter, when the rare snows hit our small Georgia town, he wrapped his shoes in burlap and trudged the entire five miles to work. His first job was sweeping the floors during second shift. For all that hard work he earned little more than ten dollars a week—after taxes, he took home only about nine dollars.

Miraculously, my parents started raising a family on that small wage. Eventually my father worked his way up and got a position as a cloth inspector—a position he held for several years, even after I was born. Fortunately, he earned a couple of raises in those first few years, but money was still hard to come by. And it was during those early years of marriage that my parents somehow learned to stretch a dollar a hundred different ways.

When my father wasn't working at the mill, he usually was either working on some project in his workshop or traveling around the countryside, preaching the word of God. After he was ordained as a Baptist minister in 1940, he began running revivals and preaching all over Alabama and Georgia. He also started writing articles—basically sermons in print—for several newspapers in the region. At one point he even had his own radio show that allowed him to spread the word of God to people he'd never met in places even farther away. It seemed my father could hardly find enough ways to spread the good news and introduce people to the Lord.

By far his most original idea was taking the word of God to the streets with a loudspeaker. After moving to Trion, my dad met a man by the name of Floyd Crowe, who was also a Baptist preacher by trade. They both did woodwork and started making picture frames together at Floyd's place in Frogtown, a part of Trion that earned its name from the way that it always flooded during heavy rains. Floyd and my father became preaching partners. They bought a tent together and began running revivals and traveling around the countryside to revive old congregations and start up new ones. They went to prisons to preach the word of God to inmates. They preached in front of courthouses. They washed people's feet and baptized new converts in ponds, rivers, and streams.

Our family in front of Aunt Betty's house, which had a little porch with a swing. My mother holds me while Earline, Gladys, and Roy Gene try to stand still for another family portrait. Aunt Betty eventually moved back to Valley Head and opened a restaurant called the Rosebud Cafe.

They basically preached the word of God everywhere they could, anywhere they could find an audience—even if two ears were all that showed up to listen.

It wasn't long after they paired up that the two men came up with a revolutionary idea: They could hold church services even if they were miles away from a church or a big revival tent. My father saved up money and bought a car with pocket change he'd diligently saved in a jar. That car basically became a traveling advertisement for God. With a paintbrush, my father wrote in white letters on the door: "The wages of sin is death. Your soul is most precious. Seek Jesus today." Once my

Dad and Floyd Crowe hold their well-worn Bibles in front of the old Chevrolet they drove as traveling preachers. My father painted religious messages on the side of the car, hoping to save people with the word of God. The car had a loudspeaker on top, which my father used as he sat on the roof and preached the word of God to people in the streets.

father finished trimming the car, he and Floyd began rolling down the streets of Trion and neighboring towns. Floyd would drive very slowly while my father sat on a platform attached to the roof of the car with his Bible and a loudspeaker. When it looked as if they had an audience, Floyd would stop the car, and my father would start preaching to children, adults, and anyone who had open ears and enough curiosity to stop and take in my father's message. Sometimes my father and Floyd drove through town to spread the word about their upcoming revivals. They drove around town, passing out fliers my father had made himself and then they'd announce

My parents stand in front of the car my father drove when he was a traveling preacher in the 1940s.

on the loudspeaker the time and date of the next tent-gathering.

However, not everyone thought this method of advertising and preaching was a good idea. The people who seemed to have the largest objection to my father sermonizing on wheels were those folks in uniform who made their living enforcing the law, keeping the peace, and keeping the streets free of loudspeakers. But usually by the time the lawmen arrived, my father had already managed to deliver a short sermon and invite people to his next tent revival. My father has always been a law-abiding man, but I guess that was one instance when he felt God's rules deserved the upper hand.

I'm not sure how my father found the time to do all the preaching he did during his first years in Trion while still holding down his job at the mill. Some Sundays he would drive from church to church, preaching as many as four different sermons in one day. I'm sure he came home hoarse on more than one occasion, because when my father delivered messages God told him to deliver, he spoke up—especially since loudspeakers weren't available in most of the sanctuaries. I think at some point, my father probably lost count of all the

My father, in the foreground on the left, stands with Floyd Crowe, preparing to baptize a large group of people in Moon Lake near Gadsden, Alabama.

churches in which he stood behind the pulpit delivering his sermons. When congregations called on him to preach, he always had a sermon ready. During his first years of marriage, he pastored a small church near Lookout Mountain in Alabama called Rock Bridge Baptist Church. I guess he was asked to preach there after word spread about his tent revivals. It was during the time at Rock Bridge that my father baptized my mother in the Little River in Alabama. My father preached at other churches, too. There was Howard's Chapel in Alabama's DeSoto State Park; a foot-washing congregation called Liberty Hill Baptist Church on Lookout Mountain; Mount Carmel Baptist Church near Fort Payne, Alabama; Berryton Baptist Church in Berryton, Georgia; and Delmar Baptist Church near Lookout Mountain in Alabama.

Around the start of World War II, my dad was preaching on a regular basis at several churches in Alabama and Georgia while the country geared up for battle. Like so many industries during that time, the cotton mill in Trion was trying to increase production to help the American troops and the country's economy. That's when the Riegel's Cotton Mill asked its employees to start working on Sundays. Dad told his supervisors he couldn't work on the Lord's day because he had two churches he was pastoring—two congregations that relied on

Religion was always a part of my family's life. My father holds a picture of Jesus for this 1942 family portrait, taken in Valley Head, Alabama, near Rock Bridge Baptist Church, one of the first churches where he preached. Earline stands next to my father, and Gladys is in front of her. My mother holds Roy Gene, who appears more fascinated with Jesus than the camera.

him to show up every Sunday and deliver their sermons. Even though working at the mill meant a regular paycheck for our family, my father felt that saving souls was a more important job that offered greater rewards having nothing to do with money. Howard Finster has always believed that if one's calling in life is saving souls, that pursuit alone should be given highest priority—not money or a regular paycheck.

Nonetheless, my father met with his supervisors at the mill to negotiate his hours. He conceded to work on Sundays in addition to preaching if they would agree to change his hours at the mill. This must have been a difficult concession for him, because he never believed in working on Sundays. But despite his willingness to bend his personal rules, he and his bosses couldn't reach an agreement about those Sunday shifts. So my father decided to quit the mill and earn his living by preaching and doing odd jobs in his workshop for people around town.

Even after I was born, my father was still traveling and preaching. I knew his work was important, but I always hated it when he left for revivals being held hundreds of miles away. Sometimes he'd be gone for several days at a time, and it would just be my mother and us children there at the house. I never really felt safe when my father was away from home. Back then, we didn't have a phone, and my mom had no weapons

My father never worried about how we looked when he took our pictures. I'm about three here, just up from a nap in church. The setting is Berryton Baptist Church in Berryton, Georgia, one of several churches where my father preached before becoming pastor at Chelsea Baptist Church.

at her disposal to protect us from danger, with the exception of a large butcher knife that she kept in one of our kitchen drawers for cutting up an occasional chicken.

I remember one time my mother took that butcher knife out of the kitchen drawer, and it wasn't to prepare dinner. My father was far away at a revival when a carload of men came up to our house wanting her to open up the grocery store below our house. It was well after closing hour, and the men were persistent, angrily knocking on our doors. I think for some reason my mother felt a sense of foreboding when those men showed up. She quickly ushered all of us children down the narrow set of steps to our grocery store on the ground floor. I rarely saw my mother show fear during all the years I was growing up. But her fear was contagious, and that night is still sharp in my mind. If I think about it long enough, even after all these years, the fear of those moments returns to me. I remember standing in the dark in silent terror with my sisters and brother, huddling closely behind my mother in our narrow stairwell. I can still see my mother with her butcher knife poised in the air, tensing and waiting for the carload of men to break into our house. Those moments stretched out into what seemed an hour as we leaned into the darkness, listening for sudden noises and signs of an imminent break-in. But we never heard the sounds of those

My mother always had her hands full when we were growing up—especially when my father traveled to faraway revivals. This picture was taken in front of my Aunt Betty's house in 1946. I'm in Mother's arms, and Gladys, Earline, and Roy Gene look shyly toward the camera.

men breaking into our house. After my mother was sure the men had left our property, we all continued down the stairs to our small grocery store to see if everything was okay. Even though we came away from that incident unharmed, my mother, sisters, brother, and I never forgot that night. Every time my father started packing to go away on another trip to some revival in a far-off city, there was an air of tension in the house, and I would feel a quiet sense of dread and unease that only subsided when he returned home.

After that frightful night, it seemed my father started cutting back on revivals that required him to venture far away from home for several days at a time. Even though God was always at the center of my father's life, I think he started growing weary of spending all that time on the road and away from his wife and children. But sometimes his increasingly frequent decisions to stay home were overruled. I remember around this time, when I was four or five years old, my father was supposed to go down to Florida for a weeklong revival near Miami. But the night before he was supposed to leave, he told my mother he had decided not to make the trip.

I imagine she was relieved to hear of my father's decision and probably fell asleep a lot more easily.

Then, at some point in the middle of the night, my father had an experience that changed his mind

My father on the beach near Miami during a two-week revival around 1949. During those two weeks, he saved twenty-two people.

and convinced him that canceling his plans to attend the revival was not what God intended for him to do. The way my father tells the story, he woke up suddenly from a sound sleep and saw someone enter his bedroom, then walk toward the foot of his bed. The figure was wearing a white gown like the one his sister Abbie had worn when she descended out of the sky over the fields in Valley Head so many years before. At first he thought it was one of us girls—I suppose because of the long, white gown. But then he realized the late-night visitor was not one of us. No words were exchanged between my father and this other-worldly guest, but my father took the visit as a divine sign that he'd made the wrong decision, that he was supposed to go to Miami after all, whether he felt like it or not. And so the next morning he packed his suitcase and left for Miami. During the revival, someone persuaded him to stay an additional week. My father agreed, and during his visit he saved twenty-two souls.

I always knew my father had thought about my mother and us children the entire time he was away from home. Whenever he returned from his trips, he'd always wake us up—no matter what the hour—showering us with little gifts and fruit he'd gathered or bought for us during his trip.

My father still ran revivals after the one in Miami, but, fortunately, they were closer to home and he often took our whole family along with him. I guess you could say my dad was still somewhat of a traveling preacher back then, but when he accepted a permanent job as preacher for Chelsea Baptist Church in 1950 he no longer had as much time to spend on the road. His focus shifted from saving souls in faraway places to firing up an old congregation. He drew new people into the church, built a community centered around God, and helped each one of Chelsea's members walk a straight path down the road to salvation.

CHAPTER 5
Building a Church;
Building a Congregation

The Chelsea Baptist Church building was about one hundred years old when my father began pastoring its congregation in 1950, and the age of the building showed. In a state of disrepair, the church leaned precariously to one side, threatening to topple over at the first sign of a strong wind. If you stood just right in the sanctuary, you could see pieces of sky glinting through cracks in the roof. I suspect my father was concerned about the safety of holding services in that building. So shortly after he became pastor, he decided to spearhead an effort to build a new church on top of the hill across the road. With my father's urging and direction, members of Chelsea Baptist Church began raising money to build a new house of worship. But the money they raised was not enough to pay for the whole project, so the congregation voted to take out a bank loan. With that money and a lot of hard labor, the people of the church began building the new structure.

Dad in front of the old Chelsea Baptist Church near Menlo, Georgia, where he began pastoring in 1950.

With much regret, my father and others in the congregation tore down the old, teetering building. Even though most were in agreement that a new one was needed, it was hard to let go of that humble, tumbledown church that had been the site of all those weddings, births, baptisms, and funerals. But the congregation was able to preserve part of the old church and all of the memories attached to it. My father, who has always believed in saving, recycling, and reusing old materials, led the effort to save part of the old church by building some of it into the new one. It helped save on building costs, and it helped members of the congregation to know that some of their memories would remain within the walls of the new church building. Once the old church was leveled, members hauled some of the wood from the walls and floor of the old church across the road to the building site. So with their hammers and nails, the congregation of Chelsea Baptist Church began building a

Shortly after Dad started working as pastor at Chelsea, he convinced the congregation to build a new church across the road. Some wood from the old building, pictured here, was used for the new structure.

new house of worship with the old wood and new timber they cut down near the church property. My father characteristically pitched in with his own hammer and nails, and after several months of diligent work, there finally was a new church the congregation could call home.

After all that work, it probably seemed unfair to some that the church didn't yet belong entirely to the congregation. Despite all those months of hammering and hauling wood across the road, the church was still partly owned by the bank, to which the congregation still owed money. I suppose for

The new Chelsea Baptist was built on a hill in Menlo. The congregation sometimes gathered for picnics on the grounds. My sister Gladys married in the church, and we attended services there three times a week.

some members, helping pay off that loan was almost as tough as digging into the hard, red clay to build the foundation for that new church. But several years and many church collection plates later, the congregation of Chelsea Baptist Church was finally able to pay off its debt to the bank.

When that happy day arrived, my father and a couple of deacons at Chelsea ceremoniously burned the bank's loan note in front of the entire congregation where the choir usually sang its Sunday hymns. I guess it was my dad's way of showing members that the church they'd built with

J. H. Willingham (left), a deacon at Chelsea Baptist, holds the note showing that the loan for the new building is paid off. My father (center) and deacon Earl Smith (right) prepare to burn the note in the choir area of the new church.

their own hands was finally paid for with all the money they'd placed Sunday after Sunday into collection plates passed among the pews.

I remember thinking as a young girl that the new church wasn't nearly as fancy as some of the mansions Dad built for us in our backyard. It didn't have a tall steeple or fancy windows with green trim like the miniature church we had behind our house in Trion. Even so, the beautiful white building served its purpose—a solid, dry house of worship that had room enough for a growing congregation. The new church was much larger than the old one.

And around the building was a thickly wooded area that provided nice shade for children playing before and after services. The new location also offered more spacious grounds outside. Surrounding the new church building were grounds big enough for outdoor church suppers, Sunday services, and weddings like the one my sister Gladys had several years after the new church was built.

Nearly everyone in the congregation was happy with the new building except for Mr. Pledger, who had always insisted on chewing his tobacco, even during services. In the old church, Mr. Pledger sat in

Gladys, Roy Gene, my parents, and I line up in front of our green Buick after a church homecoming one Sunday. Homecoming was an all-day church service with a big dinner, lots of singing, and guest speakers. At the time of this picture, Gladys was probably the church pianist.

the same seat at the front of the sanctuary every Sunday. He had permanently claimed that position on the pew because there was a hole in the floor directly below where he could spit out his tobacco juice while still appearing attentive during the Sunday sermon. But the new church floor didn't have that convenience for Mr. Pledger, and he made it known that he was not happy about the change. I suspect that Mr. Pledger was no longer able to chew his tobacco during church services. If he did continue, I am quite sure those who hammered that solid floor together made sure he wasn't spitting on their handiwork.

After he'd successfully built a new house of worship, my father turned his attention to building a larger congregation at Chelsea Baptist Church. He has always had a knack for bringing people to God—a talent he used to increase our congregation at Chelsea. He was never forceful about bringing people to the Lord, but he had a gentle charisma that drew people to him. If you got close enough to him, it was hard not to meet the Lord at the same time.

So in his quiet, persistent way, my father slowly led more people to join us in the pews. He drew people into our church in a number of different ways. One method was by basically acting as a free taxi service to church. After walking to church for so many Sundays while growing up in Valley Head, Dad wanted to make sure that a long walk didn't prevent anyone from attending services. So before each Sunday service, he left our house early and drove up and down roads in the area around the church to pick up potential parishioners who had no transportation other than

This picture was taken in 1956 on Easter Sunday, which was one of the only times we wore hats to church. Standing left to right are Gladys holding our sister Beverly, mother, and Roy Gene. I am in front at age eleven, dressed up in a new outfit and a lacy white hat.

their own two feet. Many people he picked up were children who either would have had to walk to church or didn't have parents who regularly attended Sunday services.

Dad began picking some of these children up on a regular basis, including the children of Warner and Edith Wilson. The Wilsons actually belonged to another denomination at the time, so I'm not sure how my father got started driving their children to Chelsea every Sunday. But after a time, Warner decided he'd better start going to Chelsea with his children to make sure they were behaving themselves during my father's church services. I guess Warner liked the sermons so much he just decided to stay at Chelsea, and he later decided to become a member of the

My father and friend Warner Wilson outside the Wilson home at the foot of Lookout Mountain. Dad used to pick up their children every Sunday for church. Warner eventually joined Chelsea and became the church's choir director. He had a beautiful voice.

congregation. After a time, Warner and his children were baptized by my father, and they quickly became an integral part of our congregation. Blessed with one of the most beautiful voices I've ever heard, Warner was eventually asked to be the choir director at Chelsea. Under Warner's direction, Chelsea soon had one of the best choirs for miles around. Even if people didn't come for my father's sermons, the beautiful music during our services was reason enough to walk into Chelsea's sanctuary on Sundays.

My father also had a special talent for bringing people together in a tightly knit family centered around God. He did that with our family, and he accomplished the same thing with the congregation of Chelsea during the fifteen years he preached there. Over time,

The young men's Sunday school class my father taught. Dad loved working with children and young people. He also led the children's choir at our church.

us in song, he sang along with us, waved his arms up and down to direct our voices, and smiled the entire time no matter how far off key we sang. His enthusiasm was so contagious that there was no way you could give any less than your best.

Dad started other groups in our church as well. He started a Bible study for young men in the church, providing them with some of the spiritual direction he received as a young boy from his teacher, Richard Phillips. Growing up in a church family, it was an unspoken expectation that our entire family somehow made a contribution to the church above and beyond sitting in a pew every Sunday and Wednesday. My mother taught the ladies' Sunday school class, and later, when they combined the ladies and the men, she taught the entire young people's class for six years. My sister Earline played the piano, Mother filling in on some Sundays. My sister Gladys eventually made her contribution to the congregation by playing piano every Sunday.

It's fortunate that I liked the people who attended our church, because some Sundays we were with members of our congregation

our congregation truly became like an extended family, and many people began spending time together outside of the sanctuary. Dad brought the congregation closer together by initiating many new activities and traditions. One of my favorites was singing in the children's choir—a group most of my friends and I joined. My dad always managed to make work fun, and that was certainly the case with our choir practices. Always animated when directing from sunup to sundown. Once a year, when the weather cooperated, the church would organize a "homecoming" on the grounds outside our church. The service lasted all day long, and there were guest speakers and hours of hymn singing. Afterward, the congregation socialized over a large dinner cooked by the women in the congregation, and everyone would stuff themselves full of good food on the church lawn. Members of the church eventually started a tradition in which people took turns hosting dinner for our family. The idea was that the pastor and his family would eat with different members of the congregation every week so that everyone had the opportunity to get to know

Two of the Sunday school classes my parents taught gather in our backyard after a picnic. My mother is at left in the back row, and my father is in the back row, third from the right. I sit in the first row, the second girl from the left, with Gladys to my immediate left. My mother taught the ladies' class and my father taught the men's; later my mother taught all of the young people.

them. There were also the weekly church suppers that got their start during my father's tenure at Chelsea. My parents hosted some of those dinners, and on some Sundays, they brought the entire Sunday school class, children's choir, or Bible study class home, and we picnicked in our backyard, surrounded by all of my father's mansions. Afterward, my friends and I would spend the rest of the afternoon playing in my playhouse and chasing each other around our backyard until it was time to get dressed up again and go back to church for the evening service.

The Wilsons took this picture of my family one Sunday after we'd eaten dinner at their house. This was probably Father's Day or Mother's Day, because everyone is wearing flowers.

Other Sunday afternoons, my dad packed us up in our car and took us to a nearby park or to Lookout Mountain. Back then, my parents didn't have the money to take us to ball games or to the skating rink. So my father did the best he could, treating us to an afternoon in the park and sometimes stopping at a store on the way home to buy us candy and snacks for the rest of the trip. Today children would be lucky to spend so much time with their parents. My friends often accompanied us on these afternoon excursions. Often times, my father invited a couple of older ladies from the congregation, Beulah and Annie Garner, who had never married and didn't have their own transportation. He always invited them along, because they didn't have the chance to get out of town very often. Whoever went on these Sunday afternoon trips with us usually remained in our company until that evening, when my father returned to church to preach his second sermon of the day.

I know that often many children raised under the roof of a preacher grow weary of church life. Some grow up wanting never to step foot in a church again. Maybe I was unusual, but I always enjoyed going to church. I never minded saying prayers before meals or at bedtime. And I enjoyed learning about all the books in the Bible. But I have to confess there were a couple of things I didn't like about growing up under the wing of a Baptist preacher.

Thomas E. Scanlin Collection

A member of the congregation donated a miniature white Bible like this one for each member of the young people's Bible study class. It measures just two by one-and-a-half inches.

One thing I didn't like was the requirement that we attend all funerals at our church. Watching my friends, their parents, and other relatives grieve was always extremely difficult. I learned at an early age that death was a necessary part of life, but this knowledge didn't make it any easier to witness.

I remember my first experience with death. My father had given me a baby chicken, and one day when I was playing with it, I accidentally stepped on it. I cried and held the lifeless chick in the palm of my hand. But nothing I did revived him. My father discovered what had happened and preserved the chicken for me by performing the work of a taxidermist on my small baby bird. Even still, Dad's attempt to console me only went so far. My bird was still dead. I guess I carried that experience with me when I had to attend a church funeral. I always tried to console my friends after they had lost someone, but in the back of my mind I knew there was nothing I could do or say that would revive the person they had lost. I learned at a young age that even though God has the power to work miracles, He doesn't often bring the dead back to life.

There was one other thing I didn't like about growing up in the church—the rules my father enforced on Sundays. My father was traditional in his belief that no one should work on the Sabbath. After the evening service, we would return home and my mother would fix dinner for our family. But that was about the only kind of work allowed in our house on the Sabbath. I remember when I first started learning how to embroider how frustrated I'd get on Sundays, not being able to pick up a needle until Monday morning. Looking back on it, though, Sunday nights were special family times. Sometimes my father got out his banjo or guitar and played gospel music for us. Other times, we gathered as a family around the television set, relaxing before the start of our busy weeks.

Despite those Sunday rules and having to attend funerals, I mostly liked growing up a preacher's daughter. I never tired of getting dressed up, going to meet the Lord in a church pew, and hearing my father preach the word of God. Even though we went to church three times a week, I always looked forward to hearing my father talk about the Bible and listening to his interpretations of the gospel. Some Sundays, I actually had the privilege of hearing my father's sermon more than once. On most Sunday mornings, while my mother fixed a breakfast of biscuits and gravy, Dad and I sat out on the front porch swing, listening to gospel music blaring from our television set. Sometimes I would ask him what his message was going to be for the congregation that day. Many times he'd pause for a few moments before starting to talk—almost as if he were composing his sermon in his mind at that very moment. Other times, he'd practice a message on me that had weighed heavily on his heart for a week or more. Those times when he'd been thinking about his sermon for a long time, it seemed as though he couldn't wait to get to church, stand behind the pulpit, and tell everyone about the message God was inspiring him to convey. In retrospect, though, I think my father sometimes practiced his sermons on me all those Sunday mornings to make sure I got his message and a good dose of the Bible—just in case I did not pay close enough attention in church or Sunday school that day.

On occasion, my father invited guest preachers into our church—I suppose to give young ministers the experience that so many preachers had given him when he was first starting out as a young pastor. But to me, none of their sermons ever compared to those my father delivered. He has always been a dynamic preacher, and even when I was young he was able to hold my attention like no other speaker—especially when he preached on Revelations. I think Revelations has always been my father's favorite book in the Bible because it is full of visions—just like the ones my father has seen all his life, just like the visions he paints on canvas with his paintbrush. Sometimes my father talked in church about his visions of other worlds that came to him during waking and sleeping hours—visions of serpents, spirits, Heaven, and Hell fires. Whenever he preached on Revelations, you could almost see

My father painted "Monsters of Planet Hell" in 1981.

the seven angels carrying the seven plagues, the lightning bolts, the earthquakes, the cloud of locusts, and the moon turning blood red. My father always scared me when he preached on Revelations because he made all of the visions real through his words and the urgency of his voice. It was during some of those sermons that I could vividly see the fires of Hell and the horror of the end days. If you can visualize Hell like that from a preacher's words, you know that you've got a good preacher because you can see it, hear it, and smell it, and you know beyond a doubt that you never want to end up there. My father always spoke with great urgency about the last days prophesied in Revelations, about

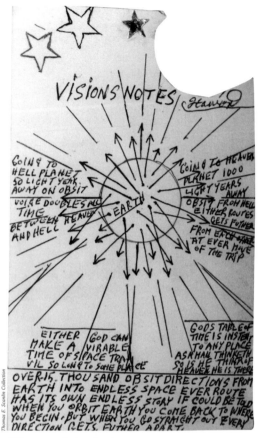

Thomas E. Scanlin Collection

When my father had a vision he would pick up something and write down his thoughts.

crying too. And if I was sitting with friends during the service, I tried to turn away to hide my tears. I guess it was pride that made me turn away like that, but as a young girl I didn't want anyone to know how strongly my father's sermons affected me.

Even though those sermons had a way of captivating me and holding my attention, there were still times as a young girl when I got distracted sitting in the hard pew during the long services. Sometimes when I sat with my friends in church, we got a little carried away passing notes and whispering back and forth among ourselves. But there wasn't much that escaped my father's notice, and when he saw that my friends and I weren't listening closely enough, he'd stop in the middle of his sermon and ask us to pay attention. That did not happen very many times because it was embarrassing to feel the full attention of the whole congregation suddenly shift from my father behind the pulpit to us girls fidgeting uncomfortably in our seats. Each time we got caught in church like that, I was convinced that punishment awaited me when my family and I got home after the service. But it never did. My father is a patient man and never had

how time was running out to save souls from damnation. Sometimes, during the delivery of his sermons, my father got so emotional about his message that he started shedding tears for all the people who still needed to be saved. Whenever he started crying during his sermons, I usually started

to say much in order to get his point across to me or anyone else.

Fortunately, I didn't get into much trouble growing up—I suppose part of that had to do with the expectations that came along with being a preacher's daughter. My father drilled it into my

My best friend Reba Garner Gill and I pose here by the side of her grandparents' home near Chelsea Baptist Church. Reba and I met at Chelsea when we were little. We still consider ourselves best friends and stay in touch. Reba still attends Chelsea Baptist Church, where she is the Treasurer.

head never to lie or steal. When I got older, he warned me against the sins of adultery, smoking, and drinking. I obeyed his wishes—not out of pressure from him, but because I always believed that he had good reasons for his advice. I guess the only time I ever strayed was when I was about twelve years old. My best friend, Reba Garner, a couple of other friends from church, and I discovered rabbit tobacco growing near Reba's house. Rabbit tobacco grows wild, and you can crush the leaves, roll them up in paper, and smoke them like a cigarette. We sneaked around a couple of times with those rabbit tobacco cigarettes. But after nearly getting caught by one of our parents, I gave up that habit for good. I remember all of us running down the road near Reba's house one time, trying to avoid getting caught. During our attempt to escape trouble, I tripped and fell, skinning both knees really badly. I remember thinking that was my punishment for going against my father's wishes. Dad found out about our misdeed, but he didn't come down hard on me. He just admonished me about trying it again and made sure I understood why smoking was a bad idea. My father was strict, but he never laid a hand on me the whole time I was growing up. He never really scolded me either. He just had this way of talking that could make you feel really guilty, a subtle way of persuading you to right your wrong the next time around. Sometimes after my father finished one of his little talks, I would almost wish I had gotten a spanking instead.

My father made this toothbrush holder in the 1940s to hang on the wall near our kitchen sink, where we brushed our teeth. Years later, I asked him to paint on the glass. Now I have angels and clouds on one of my favorite treasures.

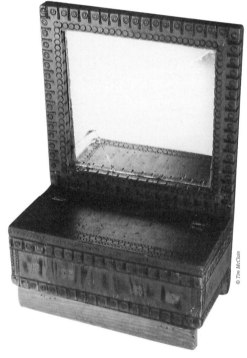

With mirrors and hinged lids, the pine hair-roller boxes my father made were quite inventive. Mom and I set the boxes on our laps in the living room Saturday night and rolled our hair for church the next day. Dad decorated them with trim similar to that which he put on his clocks.

In addition to walking a straight path and setting a good example for other children in the congregation, I was expected as a preacher's daughter to dress up a lot. Fortunately, I didn't mind wearing dresses, rolling up my hair in curlers, and getting cleaned up for church three times a week. Every night before church, I sat on one of our living room chairs or on the couch with one of the fancy hair-roller boxes my father made for us. The boxes had hinged lids, and when you opened them up, there were your hair rollers with a mirror to use when rolling your hair. By the time I woke up the next morning, I had curls for church and a choice of several dresses, most of which my mother had made.

We were always well dressed for church, even though my mother didn't have the money to buy my brother Sunday dress shirts or my sisters and me

My mother designed and made our dress patterns. Here I stand in front of her, wearing a print sundress she made for me. Gladys is in the center; to her left are Olin and Earline.

fancy dresses. I'm not sure how she did it, but my mother always made her own patterns. With her sewing machine and patient stitching, she made Sunday dresses, shirts, and everyday clothing for my brother, sisters, and me. At times my mother didn't even have the money to go out and buy fabric, so she'd improvise and use what she had on hand, which sometimes meant cotton ten-pound flour bags she bought for twenty-five cents apiece. As I grew older, my mother took some of my older

Earline and Olin met at church. Earline, in a gown Mother made, is about seventeen in this picture.

Gladys clowns around as she models her dress. In the background is our playhouse, which had a kitchen with a backdoor on it. My mother's flower bed lines the fence.

sisters' dresses apart and altered them to fit me. Often before she started sewing, she let me flip through the Sears, Roebuck catalog so I could pick out my favorite dresses. Even though she couldn't buy those outfits, my mother did her best to sew them for me by looking at the pictures and cutting her own patterns. One of my favorite dresses my mother made was mustard yellow trimmed with a small yellow print. I would often wear that dress to church, along with my fancy Sunday shoes and my little pocketbook.

The prettiest dress she ever made belonged to my sister Gladys. When my sister started playing piano for our church and in recitals, my mother got busy at her sewing machine. I guess she figured Gladys needed a dress to match her beautiful piano playing. So when my sister was about sixteen, my mother sewed her a beautiful yellow taffeta recital

Gladys, at about sixteen, sits in our Trion backyard with the museum building in the background. She is wearing the yellow piano recital gown our mother made for her.

gown. Afterward, Gladys was forever posing for pictures in that dress, beaming for my father and his camera all over our backyard. I suppose I felt a little jealous of that fancy gown, so my mother took some of the leftover yellow taffeta and made a gown just like Gladys's for one of my favorite dolls.

In all the years I spent getting dressed up to attend my dad's Sunday sermons, I never once

Gladys models the recital gown in front of a flower bed near our museum building. To her right is the playhouse; to her left is the tall cross my father made out of cement.

My doll and I are wearing dresses my mother made for us. The doll's dress, made of scraps from Gladys's piano recital gown, is in better condition than my sun dress because I was a tomboy, always getting into something and tearing my clothes. The doll is perched on the roof of one of the small mansions in our backyard.

imagined I would get saved outside the walls of Chelsea Baptist Church. I always imagined I would be listening to one of my father's sermons and wearing one of my mother's pretty dresses when that magical moment happened. But God's plan is sometimes different from the ones we wish for, and that certainly was the case the night I was saved in the middle of a crowded tent revival several miles from Chelsea Baptist Church. It happened one summer when I was about eleven years old. My family and I were attending a weeklong tent revival in Summerville, Georgia. I remember Reverend Daniels was running the revival that week, and on the night I was saved my father was standing by his side at the altar.

On that night, my mother and I were sitting in the middle of the large crowd near the back of the tent, listening to the testifying, the "amens," and the word of God coming from behind the pulpit. There wasn't really anything about Reverend Daniels's sermon that led me to the Lord that night. I suppose part of it was just the timing. But the air in that tent on that particular night was charged with a lot of God, and I guess I opened up my heart enough for some of that divine energy to touch me too. At some point I turned to my mother after Reverend Daniels's sermon and told her I felt called to the altar. My father had always told me I would know the moment I was saved, that I would know the time when God was calling me to the altar as a public profession of my faith. And as with most things, my father was right. I had always been shy, particularly around crowds. But that night, the urge to walk to the altar overpowered my shyness, and somehow I found the courage within myself to make that long trek by myself up to the front of that revival tent. My reward waited for me at the altar when I reached my father and some of my good friends. After greeting me, my father, my friends, and I prayed at the altar. Somehow in that silent moment, my awareness of the large crowd faded into the background and God took over.

Flooded with a sense of joy and peace, I walked away from the revival that night feeling like I had just grown a set of wings.

I wasn't afraid of getting saved, but getting baptized was another story. In some Baptist churches, like the one I grew up in, there's no such thing as getting a little bit of holy water dropped on

My father baptized me at age twelve in Hamby's Pond, on September 5, 1957. Posing (from left) are Nelson Wilson, me, Linda Smith, Shelby Willingham, Nancy Wilson, Marie Hammonds, my best friend Reba Garner, and my father, flipping through his Bible just before the baptism.

your head and calling the ceremony over. To get baptized in the name of the Father, Son, and Holy Ghost in our church, you had to get in the water and get wet from head to toe. Several months after I was saved in that revival tent, my father decided it was time for my baptism. Long before I was saved, my father tried to teach me how to swim in our backyard pool without any luck. And he showed me

I have always been terrified of water, but on the day I was baptized, I waded in waist deep. I knew I would be safe, because God was with me and my father was waiting for me in the pond. I am second in line in this photograph.

76

the finer points of baptism by pretending to perform the rite on me during one of my swimming lessons. Even with that early exposure to the rite of baptism, I was still nervous when it came time to undergo the real ceremony. I've always been afraid of the water, and it didn't ease my mind any to know that my baptism wasn't going to take place in a nice, clean pool like the one in our backyard. The water in Hamby's Pond was what awaited me on that day. The pond, which was not far from our church, had water so muddy you couldn't see the bottom. It didn't help to see a snake that had been killed the week before lying on the stream bank. The men in our church had spent a week preparing for our baptism day by cleaning around the pond.

When that September Sunday arrived, I stood uneasily on the edge of Hamby's Pond with the other children and adults from our congregation, listening to everyone sing "Shall We Gather at the River." I remember praying a lot as I nervously scanned the water for snakes that had been overlooked during the pond clean-up. When it was time, I gingerly stepped into the cold, waist-deep water and walked slowly toward my father in his Sunday suit, standing in the middle of the pond. When it was my turn, he held up his hand and said, "Thelma, I'm baptizing you in the name of the Father, the Son, and the Holy Ghost." Just as he had taught me, I held my breath, plugged my nose, and shut my eyes. Then my father held one of my hands, cradled the back of my head, and dipped me backward into the cold, muddy water of Hamby's Pond.

To my great relief, no snakes attended my baptism ceremony that Sunday. And even though I was baptized without incident, I was thankful when it was over.

Aside from preaching, one of my father's favorite jobs was baptizing new converts. During his time as a preacher, he not only baptized my entire family, but he also managed to baptize nearly everyone in our congregation as well. Sometimes people who belonged to other churches would ask my father to baptize them in the nearest stream or pond. A couple of times I remember him baptizing young, aspiring preachers. Even though he had started turning down opportunities to preach at revivals, I don't ever recall my father turning down the opportunity to baptize someone. To my father, baptism was a public statement of a person's commitment to Christ. In Howard Finster's mind, it was a ceremony that was just as serious and full of consequence as a wedding.

Thomas E. Scanlin Collection

This was one of the many baptisms my father performed in the Black Oak River in Fort Payne, Alabama.

For fifteen years, my father's life revolved around the baptisms, births, deaths, and lives of the Chelsea Baptist Church congregation. I think he believed he would preach at that church for the rest of his days. But one Sunday when I was in my early teens, my father received an important, silent message from the congregation—a sign that God had other plans for him. That Sunday, my father preached his morning sermon as usual. For some reason during the evening service several hours later, he decided to ask members what he had preached about earlier that day. But his question was met with an uncomfortable, leaden silence. Only one or two people raised their hands in response. Following the service, my father concluded that no one in the congregation—even the people who raised their hands—recalled the morning sermon he had worked so hard to prepare for them. He returned home that night sad and discouraged. During all my years growing up, my father was always the last person to lose hope. No matter what problem came his way—he always tackled it with hard work and faith that he'd eventually find a solution. But the problem he encountered that Sunday evening seemed to have no good solution. It wasn't something he could repair with a hammer and a few nails in his workshop. After that service, I sensed that something had changed within him, that he was fighting some battle within himself. My suspicions were confirmed only a short time later, when he announced to the members of Chelsea that he was resigning as their preacher. I think he reasoned that if members of the congregation couldn't remember his sermon after only a few hours, his continuing to preach there week after week wasn't going to do them any good either. I'm sure my father felt that he had somehow failed in the job he loved to do most, that no matter how hard he had tried to get his messages across, nothing he said was sinking in or even making a difference in their lives. After resigning from his job at Chelsea, he continued to busy himself with projects in his workshop. He has never been one to sulk or mope around. But I could tell that Trion just wasn't the same place for my father once he was no longer leading Chelsea Baptist Church.

I grew up thinking that my family and I would remain in Trion forever, living among my father's mansions. But after quitting his preaching job, my father felt there was little choice but to move on—not only from Chelsea Baptist Church, but also from the place we had called home for so many years.

My father baptized many people as a preacher. Here he baptizes a group of Chelsea members. The handwriting on the front of the picture is Howard Finster's.

79

CHAPTER 6
HE SAW BEYOND SERPENTS
TO PARADISE

By the time my father resigned from Chelsea Baptist Church, my family had outgrown our crowded acre in Trion. With all of the buildings in our backyard, my father had run out of room to build any more mansions, birdhouses, or flower beds. Shortly after leaving Chelsea, he found some property in the unincorporated community of Pennville. Just south of where we lived in Trion, the property is now considered to be part of Summerville. Some people argue that Paradise Garden is in Summerville. To me, Paradise Garden will always be in Pennville.

In any case, my father discovered this property while he was building a sunroom for a woman by the name of Mrs. Lowery. While he was building it, he took notice of the several acres of land that bordered her neatly kept house. Recently widowed and needing money, Mrs. Lowery agreed to sell some of the swampy acreage near her house to my father. Along with the land, my father bought a small house that sat on the property. The house needed a lot of renovation and repair, but that didn't discourage my father from buying it. Fixing and rebuilding things have always been among his favorite pastimes anyway.

When I found out about my father's plan to move from Trion, I begged and pleaded with him to change his mind. I could not imagine leaving everything we had behind—my playhouse, all our mansions, the museum, and our cement-block house where we had spent so many happy years. But my efforts to persuade him failed. And knowing my father, I'm not surprised. When he sets his mind on something, he's a very determined man, and there's usually no turning him back from his decided path.

This sign marked the main trail at Paradise Garden.

81

Thomas E. Scanlin Collection

THIS WAS
LAND WAS THE
ONLY PLACE I HAD
TO PLANT A GARDEN
Nonono 1983

*My father wrote this thought on a pantyhose
container and displayed it in his garden in 1983.*

So following my father's lead, my family packed up all of our belongings, left all of our empty mansions behind, and started rebuilding our lives in Pennville. Determined to build another backyard park, my father rallied the entire family to start clearing the property from years of neglect and unbridled growth. It was tough, sweaty work out there in the Georgia heat, and it seemed as though we'd never be able to dig deep enough to find a yard underneath all the weeds and underbrush. At first it was hard for me to find anything redeeming about that piece of property. With sweat dripping into my eyes and soaking through my clothes, I longed for the serenity of our already-mowed and well-manicured lawn in Trion. But my father has always seen possibilities in the oddest places, and that's what he saw when he first set eyes on those few small acres in Pennville.

At first it was nearly impossible to see what the land looked like underneath all the underbrush. It seemed that every square inch was covered with briar patches that scraped our arms and legs as we mowed, cut, and tilled our way through the thick growth. My mother rarely missed church and, to my memory up until that time, never considered skipping a Sunday service. But for the first few weeks in Pennville while we were clearing our property, my mother and I were almost too embarrassed for us to attend church because we were covered head to toe with bright-red scratches from the war we were waging against the briars. Not even the finest Sunday church dress or suit could cover all of our cuts and scratches.

Far worse than the briar patches, though, were all the snakes that had already taken up residence on our new property. They apparently were drawn to all the blackberries and the same stream that clinched the deal for my father the day he decided to buy the land. Every time Dad started running his tiller, snakes slithered up out of nowhere, their heads peering up at us over the tall underbrush. I would have been willing to tolerate a hundred more briar scratches if it had guaranteed the sudden disappearance of those snakes. But that was one prayer of mine that God never answered.

Nevertheless, I spent a lot of time praying during those first few weeks in Pennville—mostly for my safety. Already terrified of snakes, I lived in perpetual fear of getting bitten by a water moccasin or stepping on any number of the various reptiles we continued to encounter while cutting our way through the weeds and the low-lying brush. For sheer amusement and the sake of curiosity, we started counting all the snakes we killed while clearing those acres in Pennville. Once our tally surpassed eighty, we decided to stop counting. It was discouraging to think about how outnumbered we were, and I think all of us secretly wondered whether we'd ever rid the property of all that unwanted wildlife.

After the passage of several weeks, though, we were finally able to declare victory over the snakes and the briar patches. And once we had cleared the property, there was time to do so. But my father, who has always been restless and tireless when it comes to work, continued toiling away without a break. As soon as he had a cleared, mowed piece of land to work with, he began building us a new

I am seventeen in this picture, which was probably taken on a Sunday afternoon while we admired our work. We had just finished clearing the little stream that ran from a spring on the property, and Dad had built this bridge to make do until he could built a better one.

backyard park and remodeling our new house. It seemed as if he worked day and night—just like he had growing up on the farm in Valley Head. As my father worked, I slowly began to see what he had envisioned when he decided to buy the land from Mrs. Lowery.

I could not have guessed at the time that in the span of a few short years, the new backyard park my father built for us would begin drawing a flood of tourists and curiosity-seekers—not just from the towns surrounding ours—but from all over the United States. After my father's paintings appeared in various art shows, the three acres full of briar patches we cleared eventually became known to the

Overhead view of Paradise Garden around 1979.

world as Paradise Garden, an even more spectacular and unusual attraction than our backyard park in Trion had been. At the time, though, Paradise Garden was simply my backyard, not a tourist attraction. I just knew that our backyard was a little different from everyone else's and that my father never saw it as a completed project—he was constantly following one idea after the other, building the blueprints in his imagination one project at a time.

Our new backyard park bore little resemblance to the one my father built us in Trion. There were no mansions with green-and-white trim or miniature churches with steeple bells. The only building remotely similar to those mansions was the playhouse for my younger sister Beverly. It wasn't as fancy as the playhouse we had in Trion, but it had a V-shaped roof, and my father painted it white with red trim. We still had fancy sidewalks, a garden, and a lot of animals, but by the time we moved to Pennville, my father was following other plans, other projects, and making a steady progression that none of us could have predicted would lead toward his eventual fame as an artist.

My father's favorite part of our new property in Pennville was the creek. I guess you could say that Paradise Garden got its start around that trickling water. Fascinated with running water, my dad began building our new backyard park around that creek bed. He liked his water clear, and after ridding our property of briars and snakes, he began clearing that creek of debris and silt. When the water finally ran clean enough to suit my father, he began building bridges across the creek, where we could sit and dangle our legs off the edges,

Sixteen and wearing a dress I made myself, I rest on one of the bridges my dad built across a creek in our backyard in Pennville. The building in the background is our Bible House. He painted Bible messages on the outside of it.

watching all the fish, turtles, and crawfish in the water below. Dad always liked water lilies, and I suppose he figured they wouldn't grow very well in the creek. But he has always found a way around any obstacle, and he was determined to have water lilies. My father managed to rescue an old tin barrel from somewhere, which he placed near the creek. Inside the barrel, he grew his water lilies among the goldfish he bought for his makeshift aquarium.

My father planted plenty of other greenery around our yard. In the flower beds he had built out of cement and brick, my dad planted roses to brighten and scent our backyard. He even got roses to vine around the branches of some of our trees, along with all of our grapevines and wisteria. He also made sure that anyone walking through our backyard wouldn't leave hungry. During the summer months, you could start walking through our backyard with an empty stomach and leave a short while later feeling like you'd just eaten a four-course meal. Scattered throughout the yard were apple trees, plum trees, peach trees, and fig trees. And if you didn't want to snack on fruit, you picked chestnuts. My father's garden was always thriving. We never had to go out and buy green beans, tomatoes, corn, squash, or okra. All we had to do was walk a few yards from our house and pick all the vegetables we wanted for our dinner table.

Our goats, chickens, and the rabbits we raised were well fed and well housed. Our goats lived in a barn behind our house, and my dad built cages on stilts for our chickens and Angora rabbits.

Howard and a portion of the many sidewalks he created for Paradise Garden.

Winding through our backyard were fancy sidewalks, similar to the ones we had in Trion. But the sidewalks we had in Pennville glittered more brightly with gold, silver, shattered mirrors, and a profusion of colored glass. By the time we moved to Pennville, my father was no longer content with simply mixing cement with broken shards of glass— he was following the path of his imagination where everything was bigger, brighter, and several steps beyond our sidewalks in Trion. My mother and sisters and I hated breaking dishes or jewelry. But my father always looked forward to those occasions when we were on the verge of throwing something out that no longer seemed usable to us. Without exception, he found a use for shattered, broken possessions, rescuing them from a trip to the city dump. So we began handing over our broken necklaces and shattered cups, plates, and saucers to him. He'd store all of these assorted trinkets away. When he had enough of a collection, my dad would mix all the broken dishes and pieces of jewelry into cement and build a new section of our sidewalk. Eventually, all of our broken necklaces, bottles, and fine china shards were immortalized in the pathways that wound through our backyard. My father added his own touches by planting some of his mirrors, tools, tiles, and assorted building materials into our backyard sidewalks that steadily grew section by section over a period of several years. The overall effect was a long, winding mosaic that seemed to be a constantly evolving piece of artwork. In one of my favorite sections of sidewalk, my father placed beads that spelled out the names of each member of our family. In other sections, he created small pictures of elaborate mansions out of broken tile. Walking along that pathway was like combing for shells at the beach, only I rarely encountered a shell I didn't recognize.

This corner of the sidewalk shows a ledge Howard decorated using glass bottles.

Still, it was a constant process of rediscovery. With so many small mirrors gleaming in the sunlight, old jewelry pieces we had almost thrown away, and familiar pieces of dinner plates on which we had once eaten, it was easy to lose sight of where you were headed because it was difficult to take your eyes off the ground. But if you did happen to look up long enough, there were plenty of other interesting things to experience. One of the most interesting buildings my father built for our Paradise Garden was one he called the Bible House, which he built over a section of our sidewalk. It had no front or back door, so you could walk through the building as though you were walking under a covered bridge. Inside the Bible House hung mirrors and a wide assortment of antiques. He painted the building white with red trim and built awnings over each of the windows. The building earned its name from all the Bible verses my father painted on the outside of it. Even though my father was no longer preaching by the time we moved to Pennville, that urge to spread the word of God was still in his blood. And I think my father figured that anyone walking through our garden could still listen to his preaching even if he wasn't delivering God's messages from behind a pulpit anymore. If our visitors had two good eyes and the ability to read, they could leave our backyard feeling like they had just sat through a church service.

In Pennville, there were no buildings on the property to start with except for the house. So, just behind our house, which was the first entry to the park, my father built a small walk-through house with an enclosed room on each side to display his museum items. He kept a donation box outside the building, just like the one we had at the museum in Trion. The people who visited the building got their money's worth with some of the strange things my father housed in that little walk-through museum. I'm not sure where he located some of those items. Along with the antiques and tools hanging on the inside walls, he had a tumor displayed in a jar—he

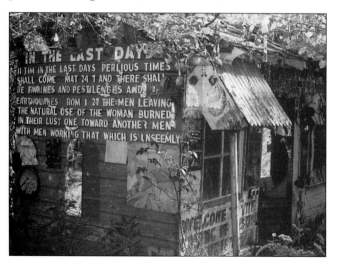

The Bible House earned its name when Howard covered it with Bible scriptures.

Howard working on the wedding-cake-shaped World's Folk Art Church. Once finished, it would contain many strange and interesting exhibits from all over the world.

had apparently persuaded a local doctor to part with it. Next to the tumor were showcased a dead snake in one jar and a dead frog in another. But one of the most popular attractions came from Gene White. After he had his tonsils removed as a little boy, Gene took care to preserve his tonsils in a jar and presented them to my father as a donation to his backyard museum. I guess my father's collection could have been housed in any Ripley's Believe It or Not! Museum. And I am sure some people walking through that building thought some of these items, such as the tonsils, were a little odd. But Howard Finster has always been just naturally curious about unusual things. Having grown up around my father's penchant for oddities, I never gave the tonsils, the tumor, or the dead snake a second thought.

Thomas E. Scanlin Collection

This "Parona Fish" made its debut in the first exhibit house my father built in Pennville.

My father had always collected things, but by the time our family moved to Pennville, he had become a real connoisseur for castaway possessions and began storing all sorts of things in various buildings around our yard. Most of his collection in Pennville originated with his desire to help people make ends meet. Sometimes they would stop by with scraps or what others might consider junk. In exchange, my father would give them money to help them out— especially if they needed the cash for food or medicine. Coupled with all the bicycle spokes, frames, and handlebars my father saved from his bicycle repair business in Trion and Pennville, our yard soon became much like the crowded, busy place we had left behind in Trion.

Apparently at a loss for what do with all of these bicycle parts, my father began piling them up in a

The Bicycle Tower at Paradise Garden.

small corner of our yard. Over time, the pile grew and grew. It started out looking like an ordinary junk pile, but nothing close to Howard Finster stays ordinary for long. I couldn't have guessed it at first, but my father eventually turned that pile of bicycle parts into an odd little structure that you could walk into. He eventually called it his Bicycle Tower, and it stands today in Paradise Garden in the exact spot where he began tossing all those parts in that haphazard fashion years ago.

90

he decorated with pieces of broken glass and a red tin roof. If the sun hits it just right, looking through that building is like looking through a stained-glass church window. Like most of my father's buildings, this one served a purpose. Inside was a pump that pulled water from the creek in our backyard, and my father called it our Bottle House.

My father built another unusual structure that still stands in Paradise Garden. He poured leftover cement into a tall mound and sculpted serpents with eyes all over the sides. The serpents are like

Top of the Bicycle Tower at Paradise Garden.

Dad also saved all of our "coke" bottles. Though none of us could imagine why, it soon became apparent that he'd drafted a use for them from the start. After he had saved hundreds of bottles, my father cemented them together into a small building

The view inside the small building built from used glass "coke" bottles.

91

The serpent mound in Paradise Garden.

The wedding-cake-shaped World's Folk Art Church.

three-dimensional versions of the snakes he had seen in some of his visions and later began painting in his artwork.

We had other backyard attractions, too. When the wind blew, the yard truly came to life. From tree branches, my father started hanging some of the items he'd collected at the dump or picked up while walking down the road near our house. He loved to hang small pieces of mirrored glass from buildings so he could watch the sun hitting them on a windy day. In our front yard, my father placed a turbine vent on a pole. He cut out tin horses and attached them to the vent. When the wind blew through the turbine, it would spin round and round like a

Our front yard in Pennville. Dad mounted a turbine vent on a pole and attached tin horses to it. When the wind blew, the horses flew around the pole like a merry-go-round. He liked to hang things that turned or blew in the wind. In the background is the sunroom he built for Mrs. Lowery, from whom we bought the property and who was like our grandmother when we moved to Pennville.

miniature merry-go-round. We had a lot of shining, spinning things like that in our yard.

I never minded that my father collected all the things he did, because I knew he'd eventually find some use for each and every item he rescued. But my mother used to get disgusted with my father for bringing home so many things that didn't seem to have an immediate use. "Howard," she'd say, "we don't need any more junk." But my father has always been so used to saving things that my mother has never managed to reform him. I guess it's a good thing because all that "junk" made Paradise Garden the magical place it was.

Howard looks through old TV sets, searching for the "perfect" one to convey his next message.

93

CHAPTER 7
MY FATHER'S VISIONS OF TIME

Thomas E. Scanlin Collection

When we moved to Pennville, I don't think my father knew exactly what he wanted our backyard park to look like. I think he began building our park much the same way he started on any project—following one idea after another. But for my father, no project is ever really complete or finished, and he continued to build Paradise Garden during all the years he lived there. During those early years in Pennville, he also spent hours at a time behind his workbench.

When my dad was not working in our backyard, I usually could find him in the workshop he and I built together at the edge of our property. A long building, it was much more spacious than his workspace in Trion. He converted the back of the building into his workshop, which was where he kept his workbench, all his tools, and his wide assortment of

We made large, medium, and small clocks in our Pennville workshop in the late 1960s. Here's one of the larger clocks my father made to sell.

woodworking machines. But with so much space, he decided to turn the front of the building into a small store that he named Howard Finster's Item Shop. Soon, that store was bustling with business.

After we moved to Pennville, my father continued painting and rebuilding bicycles. But gradually, his focus shifted to other projects. His most successful business revolved around clock-making, and soon everyone in our family was pitching in because my father couldn't build them fast enough to keep up with customer demand. I'm not sure how he started making his clocks. Like most things he built, the clocks seemed to come straight out of his imagination, because he'd never seen anything like them before—and for that matter, no one else had either. Looking back, it almost seems as though God was drawing up the

One of the large clocks my father made in Pennville.

blueprints in my father's head, and it was simply my father's job to build what he saw from the pictures that appeared behind his mind's eye. I was about seventeen years old when my father started his clock-building business. As in Trion, I was right by his side, helping him out with little jobs he gave me.

When building his clocks, my father's first step was always visiting local drugstores and department stores to find every last clock face available. It wasn't unusual for him to walk out of a store with every clock they'd stocked on their shelves. Some of the clocks were windups, others were powered by electricity, but all of them turned out a lot fancier after my father was through with them. After his shopping excursions, he would return to his workshop with those bags full of ticking clocks and begin building elaborate frames for every last one of them. For this job, my father invented several machines that cut intricate patterns into the wood trim. Later, he would glue these intricate pieces of wood onto all of his clock frames for decoration.

My father's clocks not only kept time, but also, by the time he finished with them, they had been transformed into beautiful works of art. On many of the clock frames were beautiful flowers, circles, and

A sampling of clock patterns we made only two or three times. The unusual bowl (middle) is probably one of a kind.

The larger clocks were the most popular. All of my father's clocks were cut from the same pattern, but no two ever turned out alike. I used to help shellac and make the trim. During a three-year period, our family made hundreds of clocks.

diamond-shaped patterns made with his wood-burning machine. Below some of the clock faces, my father built in small frames where people could place family photos or artwork. That way, he figured, people not only could keep track of the hours and minutes passing by, but they could also be reminded of their loved ones at the same time.

My father built a handful of large grandfather clocks that towered well above any of us, but most of his clocks came in three basic sizes. The larger clocks, which were our most popular, sold for twenty-five dollars apiece. The smaller ones we sold for twelve to fifteen dollars. In recent years, I've met some people who began collecting my father's clocks, and

Above are some of our best-selling clocks. When we made these clocks, I was married and lived across the street from my parents. My daughter Stephanie played in her playpen in the workshop while I shellacked clocks for fifty cents apiece.

they tell me it's not unusual for them to sell for more than three hundred dollars now. The most amazing thing about my father's clocks is that he never built any two alike. About the only thing the clocks have in common is a small final touch my father put on the bottom of every one before gluing on the base. I guess it was his way of blessing the person who bought one of his clocks, but he would always write "Jesus Saves" in a hidden place on the bottom of his clock frames. Dad told me he hoped that if the clock ever broke perhaps someone would find the message inside.

This grandfather clock stood about five feet tall and had a cabinet underneath. On both sides were wooden bowls made by stacking rings of wood. People bought these bowls to display items such as fruit or flower arrangements.

As with most things my father set his mind to do, his clocks soon became a great success. Before long, the whole family was involved in one way or another with my father's business. A couple of years after he started his clock-making business, I had gotten married and moved into a house across the street from my parents. It was a convenient setup, because I only had to take a short walk across the street to get to work in the mornings. I'd cart my daughter Stephanie over to my father's workshop, place her in a crib near our workspace, and then toil away with my father on those clocks all day long. I probably could have gotten a better-paying job somewhere else, but no wage would have been high enough to draw me away from my father's workshop or leave behind the chance to work by my father's side all day long.

When I was a young girl in Trion, my father's workshop was the place I preferred to be most days, because it meant I had more time with him. Even as a young mother, I felt that my dad's workspace held the same magic for me that it had when I was a little girl. We worked together better

© Tim McClain

This is one of my father's more unusual clocks. It stands about twenty inches tall, and the wood is burned to an almost black color. This clock, which is about twenty-eight years old, belongs to my son Jon.

than most business partners and soon had set up a whole system. While my father assembled the clocks with his hammer and nails, I put a coat of shellac on the ones he had finished building. He paid me about fifty cents per clock. That wage may not sound like much, but you couldn't put a price on my father's company or the satisfaction I got from watching his business grow into a huge, booming success. My mother and other members of the

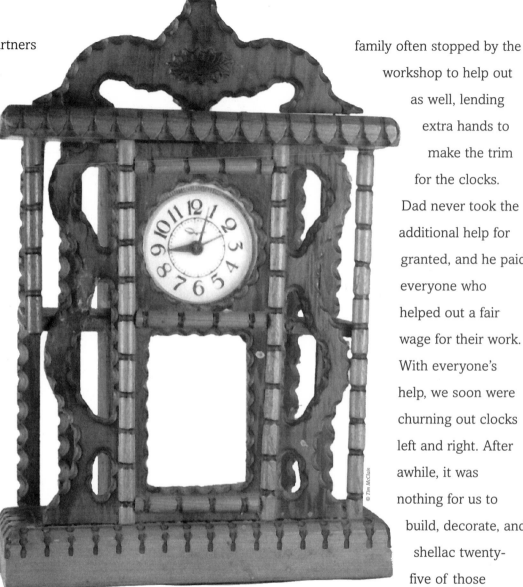

This clock, which belongs to my daughter, has a five-by-seven picture frame below the face. Before my father glued the bases on his clocks, he wrote "Jesus Saves" on them. I don't think he ever made anything without putting a little bit of God into it.

family often stopped by the workshop to help out as well, lending extra hands to make the trim for the clocks. Dad never took the additional help for granted, and he paid everyone who helped out a fair wage for their work. With everyone's help, we soon were churning out clocks left and right. After awhile, it was nothing for us to build, decorate, and shellac twenty-five of those clocks from start to finish during the course of one day.

The original clock still runs in this thirty-year-old piece. The wood has a natural finish with a leaf pattern.

Even with everyone in the family pitching in, though, there were times when it seemed we still didn't have enough hands to do the work fast enough. I'm not sure how this happened, but there was a man by the name of Mr. Thornburg who eventually found out about my father's clocks. Before long, Mr. Thornburg began making regular trips to my father's shop, driving all the way in his big truck from his home in Indiana. When he made the trip to Pennville, it was nothing out of the ordinary for Mr. Thornburg to buy thousands of dollars worth of our clocks so he could haul them above the Mason-Dixon Line and sell them to all his customers. Those clocks must have sold like

A sampling of the many types of woodwork from my father's workshop: a wooden wagon, a log cabin, a toy cannon, a small spinning wheel, one of his bowls, and a mantle clock.

Dad built many of his own machines to make trim for decorating doll furniture and other woodwork. The detail on this dresser was burned into the wood. Doll furniture always sold quickly—at Christmas he couldn't build it fast enough.

On the left is a large wooden bowl decorated with rows of trim made on my father's homemade wood-cutting machine. About fourteen pieces were glued together to make this bowl. The small clock on the right contains two picture frames.

hotcakes up there, because it seemed like every time we turned around, Mr. Thornburg was calling us on the phone to announce his next trip to Pennville. It was right before those trips when we were the busiest. Sometimes most of our family, including my mother and my husband, would be racing against time to get all the trim ready to put on clocks before Mr. Thornburg arrived in Pennville. Some of those nights I found myself wishing it were possible to grow two more arms, but somehow we

One of the toy cannons my father made in the early 1960s. He made the barrels of these guns with a turning lathe and always put wheels on them. They sold quickly at flea markets.

always managed to finish all of our work before that big truck rolled into our driveway.

It may sound hard to believe, but even in the midst of my father's clock-making, he somehow managed to find the time to build other things, too. From his homemade machines, he also churned out hundreds of fancy wooden bowls, cups, jugs, bookcases, quilt boxes, and dozens of other

103

The bowl on the left resembles a toy wagon with its whimsical wheels. Also pictured is a wooden bowl on a pedestal on top of the wagon, a wooden bottle, and another bowl on a pedestal. Unfortunately, my father hasn't done woodwork like this since the 1970s. He spends most of his time painting.

interesting items. For children, he built little stagecoaches, toy wagons, cannon guns, and doll furniture. Of those items, doll furniture was probably the most popular. He would build whole living room suites for dolls and sell them in his shop for $1.49. He'd craft fancy twenty-inch doll beds that sold for $1.98 apiece. Almost any piece of furniture you can imagine, my father made for little girls and their dolls. Around Christmastime, he worked as hard as one of Santa's elves, trying to keep all that doll furniture stocked on the shelves of his shop. Invariably, he could never seem to make enough doll furniture and we usually sold out before the end of the Christmas shopping season.

Thomas E. Scanlin Collection

The plaque on this model of a wooden stagecoach reads: "Woodcraft by Howard Finster. The Coach of Shiloh." The coach's doorknob is a thumbtack; the door hinges are leather straps. Such adornments are typical of my father's models, although this piece is unique.

© Tim McClain

Little more than two inches tall, these wooden cups are made of layers of wood glued together. Stamped on the bottom of both is "Jesus Saves." Tulips line the bottom edge of the cup on the left.

© Tim McClain

One of my favorites, this wooden bowl with a lid is lined with small flowers burned into the wood. I have used it as a thread container, and my daughter took it to college and kept her belts in it. He only made one piece like this.

My father loved to save things. He found this postcard, which was dated 1911 from the Bank of Menlo, a small community outside Summerville. He mounted the card on a wooden plaque and coated it with shellac.

A one-of-a-kind wooden bottle made out of layers of wood trim. The lid is attached with a chain. This piece is about thirty years old.

This bookshelf holds several examples of my father's craftsmanship. Among them, on the third shelf, are small wooden oil lamps he made with his turning lathe. On the left is a rocking chair also made in his workshop.

My father sometimes packed up his woodwork on the weekends and took it to Collinsville or Scottsboro, Alabama, to sell at trade days. He sold a lot of doll furniture, toys, and miniature cannons that way. Here I pretend to be in the driver's seat of our green Buick, eagerly waiting to leave town on a selling trip.

My father managed to sell quite a bit of his handiwork from the aisles in his store. But on occasion, he filled his car up with all of his clocks, doll furniture, and other woodwork, and headed to Collinsville or Scottsboro, Alabama. Both towns were known for their huge flea markets and large weekend sales, and people routinely came from miles around to buy up all the treasures they could find. Hundreds of vendors arrived at these sales to pedal their goods. Most who set up there, including my father, did a brisk business. Sometimes I accompanied my father on these trips. In order to get a good, well-trafficked spot, we usually left the night before and then slept in the car, wedged in between all my father's woodwork. We never stayed long at those sales and flea markets, because generally before the day got its start, he sold everything he'd packed so tightly into our car. After selling everything we brought with us, we returned home with an empty car and a lot of crisp dollar bills.

Thomas E. Scanlin Collection

On this Scottsboro, Alabama, trade day in 1966, Howard made three hundred dollars from the sales of his wooden treasures.

Growing up, I always thought that everything my father did, everything he created, everything he dreamed and made real eventually turned into money. From his workbench, Dad managed to create a comfortable income for our family. He continued his woodworking business for years.

109

CHAPTER 8
VACATIONS TO HEAVEN:
CASTLES ON THE BEACH

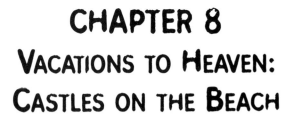

Sand Museum Draws Crowd At Gulf Beach

The creative ability of a vacationing Chattoogan recently caused a "sensation" on a sandy beach of Florida's gulf coast.

When Howard Finster, Route 2, Summerville, took his family (including eight grandchildren) for a vacation to Clearwater, he had no idea that he and his "helpers" would end up on TV and in the newspapers. But that's just what happened.

The cause of all the excitement was a sand "museum" created by Finster and his "mass of boys and girls from many states as helpers."

"We molded the structures by hand, halfway between the Flamingo Motel and the rolling Clearwater tides," he recalled. "The day before we arrived at Clearwater, the tides were breaking 50 feet beyond where we built the castles."

Continuing, Finster said: "In the beginning, we molded a large cross of Jesus, and the tide dropped back about 100 feet, remaining there steadily for six days. Thus, our sand castle museum was saved."

GULF VIEW

The Finster party occupied four full apartments. From the breakfast table, he related he

was still standing," he recalled. "That is, everything except the Tower of Babel. The children and I had a free-for-all party on

this mound of sand—flattening it out, playing and running up and down on it."

HOWARD FINSTER AND 'HELPERS'
Attract TV Cameras

Thomas E. Scanlin Collection

My father's thriving bicycle and woodwork business allowed us luxuries we'd never had during all our past years. My father managed to save nearly everything he earned from his business. Despite all that money he began making, we continued living a frugal lifestyle. We always ate the vegetables from our garden and wore the clothes my mother made until we'd either outgrown them or worn the fabric too thin for wear. Then one year—after having lived so many years on the bare bones of necessity—my father apparently decided that we had enough money to start spending it on things we'd always thought were reserved for the rich. That year, when I was about thirteen years old, my father treated us to our first family vacation. I had never ventured more than a few miles beyond our house. The only long-distance trips we took were to occasional far-off church revivals or to mountainside parks that were reachable by car in the span of one afternoon. During the first years of my childhood, the circumference of my world was a small place, and the world beyond was a sphere I was only able to visit in daydreams. But my world changed the year my father announced he wanted to take us to Florida. After that first trip, all the maps I'd studied in school suddenly became real, and I knew without a doubt that there were other states, other worlds for me to explore beyond the boundaries of Georgia.

It only took that one vacation for our family to get hooked on Florida, the sight of the ocean and all the white sandy beaches. Every year afterward, we saved our money for our Florida trip and waited with great anticipation for that day when we would back out of the drive and leave the state of Georgia for several days. Most years we waited

Resort brochures Howard picked up on his many trips to Florida. Many are from other garden attractions, perhaps to get ideas for his own garden.

111

until August, when the majority of tourists had returned to their everyday lives, leaving the beaches, zoos, and all the vacation spots less crowded. On that long-awaited August morning, my father would see to it that we had the road to ourselves for the first leg of our trip. Somehow, he always managed to rouse everyone out of bed before daybreak, and by six or seven in the morning, we'd be backing out of the drive and on our way to Florida by sunrise.

En route to Florida every year, we stopped at the Atlanta Zoo. We are taking a break here after walking through the zoo. Left to right are my mother, Beverly, me, and my father, who is waving the Rebel flag over my head.

Invariably, our first stop on these Florida trips was the Atlanta Zoo. It was at the zoo that my father truly became like a child again, running along with us children from one animal exhibit to the next. Our favorite stop was always the monkey exhibit.

Ignoring the zookeepers' stern signs warning visitors not to tap on the glass, my father would have all the monkeys swinging from branch to branch, and jumping up and down in varying degrees of agitation. After he had succeeded in exciting the monkeys, Dad would start aping their every move. Jumping up and down, he would mimic their facial expressions, scratch under his arms, holler and hoot back to the monkeys trapped on the other side of the glass. My father's monkey routine always made me laugh until my stomach hurt and I could barely catch my breath. Every year when we'd stop at the zoo on our way to Florida, my father would do a repeat performance of this routine. My mother would always do her own repeat performance, adding to the hilarity of my father's antics. She'd tug or yank on his shirt-sleeve at some point during his routine, trying to make him stop the spectacle he was creating outside the monkey cages. "Howard!" she'd say in a loud whisper, "Howard, stop it right now! You're going to get us kicked out of here!" Fortunately, we never did get kicked out of the Atlanta Zoo. And every year when we stopped there, I would eagerly rush to my favorite exhibit so I could watch my father ape the monkeys all over again.

After our stop at the zoo, we'd all pile back into the car, and my father would continue driving us down that long, winding trek to Florida. My father never believed in rushing anywhere, and the speedometer in our car always reflected his belief. Unlike most vacationers looking for the straightest, fastest route to their destination, he didn't like traveling the interstate. I eventually came to realize that, had we taken the main highway, we would have missed all of the antebellum mansions, the roadside fruit stands, the little country stores, and all the main streets with solitary red lights that dotted our route to and from Florida every year. If my father spotted an interesting building or roadside attraction on our journey, he'd put on the brakes and get out of the car. After satisfying his curiosity by nosing around these out-of-the-way places for several minutes or taking pictures, he'd usher us back into the car, and we'd continue our forward crawl down to Florida.

My father looks deep in thought outside an old Tallahassee, Florida, hotel he thought looked interesting. He's about forty-four in this picture. We always took the back roads on our vacations so we could explore different areas.

During those long miles, my father always tried to keep our boredom at bay and everyone in the car entertained. Sometimes on those less-traveled backroads, he'd zig-zag back and forth across the center line like someone who'd tasted too much moonshine. He'd do other crazy stunts, too, transforming our car into a makeshift amusement ride until my mother started her usual protests. "Howard," she'd say, "stop it. You're going to get us all killed." My father has always listened to my

Mother and Dad in front of the Flamingo Apartments in Clearwater Beach, Florida. We liked staying there, because it was right on the beach. Even now we sometimes stay at this hotel when we go to Florida. My parents were in their early forties when this picture was taken.

mother, and so he'd return to his usual slow, responsible driving, looking for some other amusement to help us while away the hours in the backseat of our car. Sometimes, in the absence of the car radio, my father would start singing loud, bellowing songs from behind the steering wheel, urging us to join in his raucous refrains. Despite his attempts to keep us children entertained, though, the main attraction for me along those winding backroads was always Florida. As a young girl, I often grew impatient to see the beach as my father made his slow, unhurried way down to Clearwater or St. Augustine.

It never mattered whether we had motel reservations or not—our first stop once arriving in Florida was always the beach. One year I remember my father seemed just as impatient to reach the shoreline as we were. Back then you could actually drive your car right onto the sand. So once the ocean was finally in view, that's exactly what my father did—he drove our car onto the beach. Unfortunately, we got stuck. So for a while my father heaved, shoved, and pushed our loaded-down car back and forth until a nice man came by and pulled us out with a chain hooked to his car. I think that year was the last time my father drove the car onto the sand like that. Even so, he was always eager to reach the beach.

Looking back on it, I'm not sure who was usually more excited to arrive at the oceanside—us children or my father. As soon as the car stopped rolling, we quickly unpacked our pails, shovels, and innertubes, climbed as fast as we could into our bathing suits, and then raced each other to the shoreline. My father always was one of the first to jump into the waves; then he would retire on the beach so he could begin building his elaborate sand castles. I think he actually enjoyed building them more than we did. And without a doubt, he was a better craftsman, too. I'm convinced he built up some kind of play deficit plowing all those fields as a young boy. He more than made up for all those years during our family vacations to Florida. All those sand castles my father never got a chance to build when he was growing up, he built during those long afternoons on the beach. He literally spent hours crafting his fancy sand mansions, molding all that wet sand into spectacular shoreline cities.

Every year without fail, he remained planted there, losing track of all the hours he'd spent under the blazing sun. After a couple of those trips, we came to realize that going to Florida would mean my father would get his annual sunburn. He never complained about much, but we definitely heard him groaning about his burning red skin and the chills he had while trying to fall asleep in our

Howard obviously enjoying swimming in the ocean on one of the family trips to St. Augustine.

Florida motel room. My mother was always a little bit more practical when it came to the hours spent on the beach, and she would stay sheltered in the shade for most of these afternoons. I never saw her wear pants—or a swimsuit for that matter. Even at the beach, she always wore a dress, and she only wore shorts and a blouse to go into the water. After most of our vacations, she was the only family member who returned from Florida without the skin peeling off of her shoulders.

I was much older and had my own family the year my

My children, Stephanie and Jon, helped my father build this row of sand castles along Clearwater Beach in 1970. Dad was an attraction on the beach that year because of all the intricate castles he built in front of the Flamingo Apartments, catching the attention of the local television stations and newspapers.

father built a long line of sand castles that stretched in an elaborate display down the beach. The sand castles attracted the attention of almost every child on the beach, including my children. My father soon found himself flanked by a small army of helpers eager to replenish buckets of water and oversee his progress while he built his magical castles. That year, my father's handiwork also attracted the attention of many adults. Word quickly spread about the sand city he built in a few short hours. Before long, reporters from the local news media were dragging their heavy cameras and equipment across the sand to interview my father. That night in our motel room, we watched my father's beaming face on the nightly news as he basked in the sudden attention he had earned for his artistic endeavors on the beachfront that day. Unlike my father, my mother has never enjoyed the spotlight or large crowds, so while my father was enjoying his brief moments of local fame, my mother was hugging the background somewhere in the shade.

When Dad wasn't building sand castles, he was combing the beach for new finds. He'd hunt along with us for interesting shells and rocks tossed onto the shore by the waves. He had a good eye for the unusual, and we'd always leave Florida with pocketfuls of odd-shaped stones and shells filled with sand. Then, after buying a metal detector, his favorite beachside pastime became combing the sand for hidden treasures. He'd find necklaces, old coins, and bottle caps tossed away by careless visitors.

Jon sits on top of a large sand alligator at Clearwater the same year my father was on the news. Behind Stephanie is a snake the three of them built out of sand.

Though many of his finds didn't have much monetary value, I think he continued to hope that one day he'd hit gold during one of his beachside treasure hunts.

The afternoons we spent on the beach were always among the highlights of our vacations.

But we regularly visited other sites, too. And once we discovered a new attraction, we would return year after year like a small flock of birds gravitating to familiar territory. One place my father grew fond of was St. Augustine. Unlike so many Florida vacation spots, St. Augustine didn't draw big crowds. Compared to Jacksonville and Daytona, St. Augustine wasn't crawling with tourists—that's just the sort of place where my father liked to find refuge. He was drawn there because it was a relatively quiet historical town. His favorite stop was the old Spanish fort, Castillo de San Marcos, that we invariably explored year after year. My father would walk past the old, crumbling walls of the fort, making up stories about all the prisoners he imagined had once lived there. Being his child, I found it difficult not to get interested in

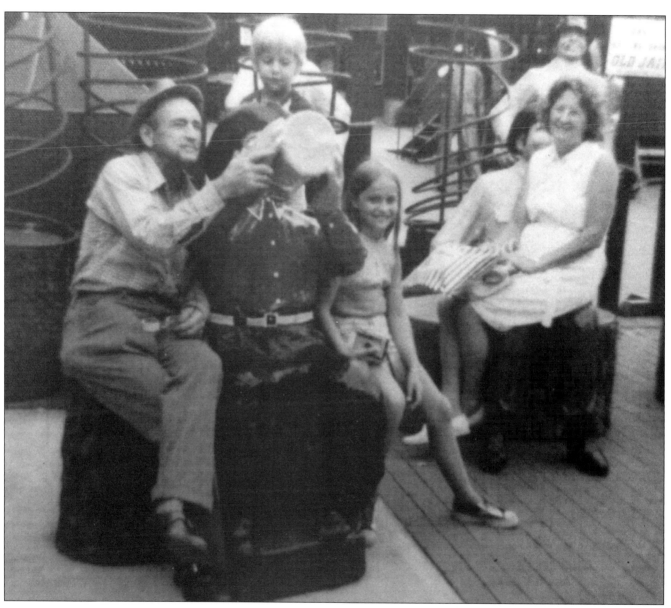

My father pretends to hold a whiskey jug for a mannequin outside the Old Jail in St. Augustine. My mother sits on another mannequin on the far right. Jon and Stephanie always got a kick out of anything their grandfather did.

history, because he always tried to make it come alive in our minds with his tall tales. On one of our trips, we discovered a place called Marineland—a large aquarium between St. Augustine and Daytona. We stopped there every year afterward, and my father would try to attract the attention of the fish—just like he did the monkeys at the Atlanta Zoo—by tapping on the glass and making funny fish faces. Then my mother would get disgusted just like at the zoo, and the rest of us would have a good chuckle watching my father break the rules.

While he enjoyed the old Spanish fort in St. Augustine and Marineland, my father's favorite stop was the Ripley's Believe It or Not! Museum. We didn't go there every year, because it would take my father hours to walk through the entire museum. He'd stop and marvel at each unusual display, reading all the signs and returning to all his favorite exhibits. Our feet sore and curiosity long gone, we'd all have to practically beg my father to walk out the doors of that museum. During all those visits to Ripley's, I think my father was collecting some new ideas for his own museum in our backyard in Pennville. After we started going to Florida, my father's collection of oddities grew. In addition to his nephew's tonsils and that snake in a jar, he had been acquiring other strange things for

My father leans on a cannon at the old Spanish fort in St. Augustine. I think he got the idea for building his toy cannons from our visits to this site. We started vacationing in St. Augustine when I was about fifteen. My mother, Beverly, and I are in the background.

Dad clowns around as a deep-sea diver outside Marineland. We went there every year to look at the aquariums.

his collection—including the remains of an unknown girl who had been buried in a shallow grave underneath an old house in Trion.

Most years before leaving for Florida, we planned months ahead for our departure, deciding where we would stop along the way and our entire itinerary. One particularly memorable year, we got up one morning with no knowledge that we'd be headed to Florida within the span of a few short hours. Our original plans that morning were to drive to Valley Head to visit my father's sister at his old homeplace. But during our short drive to Valley Head, all of us started daydreaming aloud about our next Florida vacation. As it turns out, we didn't stay in Valley Head for long. The more we talked about Florida, the closer we came to going. Dad was counting the hours it would take to get us there. By the time we got to my aunt's house we were borrowing clothes from her to take to Florida. Headed south with little else but the clothes we put on that morning, we drove all the way to Florida that day. We didn't stay our usual week at the beach. But that hardly mattered. Of all our trips to Florida, that impromptu vacation stands out more than most of the others combined. And it's one of the best examples I can think of when I try to explain what an adventure it was growing up with my father.

I learned a lot of life lessons working by my father's side in his workshop and listening to his sermons. But it wasn't until I was much older that I realized just how much I had learned about life and journeys from him during those long family vacations. I learned that having only one destination in mind is a sure way to miss out on the majority of what life tries to reveal to you through sudden turns, dips, and jags in the road. Thinking back on all those Florida trips, I came to realize that taking the backroads sometimes leads you to places others miss while driving their hurried pace down main highways. Traveling the main routes on a journey may get you to your destination faster, but it's the slow, winding backroads in life—those places where few choose to travel—that often lead to the best discoveries, the most unusual experiences, and the richest journeys.

Most important, I eventually realized during those vacations that, no matter how old you are, it is imperative to keep the playground in your mind alive. It's important to keep the child inside yourself alive by breaking the occasional rule, teasing monkeys, swinging on swings, spinning on merry-go-rounds, sliding down slides, coloring outside the lines, and building sand castles—even if they aren't anywhere near a beach.

One of my father's favorite stops on our Florida journeys was the Ripley's Believe It or Not! Museum in St. Augustine. He had to walk through and look at everything. He took this picture around 1960 of me, my mother, and Beverly.

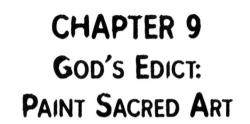

CHAPTER 9
GOD'S EDICT:
PAINT SACRED ART

Even after I was married and had my own family, I continued traveling to Florida with my parents every year with my husband and children in tow. During those years, my father continued selling his woodwork and fixing bicycles. When I had time to spare I was by his side, helping him with his woodworking projects. But after years of watching my father start and run his successful businesses, I soon became eager to start my own venture and began running a small fabric store in downtown Trion. I enjoyed it, but my store didn't possess the same magic I found in my father's workshop. This became especially clear to me one day in particular. To my knowledge, God never visited my store to buy a piece of fabric. But from what my father tells me, God walked right into Dad's workshop one afternoon and bought the rest of his working days.

This early painting of William Shakespeare is titled "Clost To Howards First Art." "My First Art" is painted over at the top. Howard started numbering his work shortly after this piece.

As my father tells it, he was in the middle of painting a bicycle when it happened. He was touching up a patch on a bicycle frame with white paint and glanced down at one of his fingers in the middle of the job. There on the round tip of his finger and centered in white paint, my father saw the image of a human face. My father sat looking at his fingertip in wonderment for a few moments and then felt a familiar feeling wash over him. It was the same kind of warm feeling he had had the night he was saved in that revival tent outside Violet Hill School. It was the same feeling he'd had at three when he saw his sister descend from the clouds above his farmhouse. And it was the same feeling he had in Trion when a spirit visited him in the middle of the night, convincing him to go to the weeklong revival in Miami. This time, sitting alone in his workshop, my father knew that he was about to get a visit from another world. He waited for several moments in silence, staring at the face on his fingertip, and then he heard a familiar voice speaking to him.

"Paint sacred art."

Stunned, my father sat in the quiet space of his workshop for several moments, contemplating God's odd edict. After several moments, my father responded. My father answered that he could not do what God was asking, that he had no training to paint anything other than bicycles, houses, and little backyard mansions. After a couple of moments, the voice returned with a simple question.

"How do you know?"

Dad sat on that question for several moments and then realized that he didn't have a good answer. During all the years in his workshop, he had always

An easel board my father gave me in the 1980s. I recently took it to him to sign. Little did I know he would paint faces all over it and turn it into an unusual piece of artwork. He made all his own easel boards. This one apparently saw lots of use, as the bottom right leg is worn down.

figured out how to do all the things he started out not knowing how to do. He'd always said yes to any project that came his way, whether he started out knowing how to do it or not. So he had no choice but to find an answer to that challenging question God posed to him in his workshop that afternoon. My father knew after that afternoon visit that he was expected to at least try what he thought he couldn't do. So my father took a dollar bill out of his wallet, tacked it onto a piece of plywood, and decided he would try to draw the face of George Washington. My father started out thinking he was going to show God that He'd picked the wrong man for the job. But by the time he finished drawing, he realized God was right. He could draw and paint after all. So on that day, my father accepted the job God had offered to him and he started painting himself down a path that would transform the rest of his life.

After God called my father to paint sacred art that afternoon, it seemed as if my father had undergone some kind of second conversion. It was almost as if he'd gone away to some tent revival and returned with a paintbrush in his hand. I think God handed my father an opportunity that afternoon in his workshop because He knew my father would paint the visions he'd witnessed all of his life. God knew that along with paint and water, my father would stir some of his preaching into the mix, brushing all of it together in bright, beautiful colors, sweeping his visions of Heaven across one canvas after another. I am certain that God called on my father that afternoon, knowing that my father would paint the way to salvation for thousands of souls he'd never had the opportunity to save during all his years behind the pulpit. Baptized by a growing fire in his imagination, my father began preaching through his paintbrush, delivering the promise he had made to God that afternoon in his workshop.

Photo © Tim McClain

Thomas E. Scanlin Collection

My father painted this landscape picture and gave it to me when I was fifteen. He didn't start painting until much later, but the talent was always there. He also made this frame.

With God looking over his shoulder, everything in my father's life soon became a canvas. Just as it had been with his clocks, it seemed my father could hardly paint his pictures fast enough. Early in his painting career, he didn't bother spending money on

This large painting on canvas hung in Paradise Garden.

My father would use just about anything to record his messages. This old camper stills sits in Paradise Garden.

fancy art supplies or special paint. Just as he had always done, Howard Finster used what he had on hand. The visions my father had carried around in his mind for all those years suddenly began taking shape throughout our backyard. In bright colors, he began painting all over the buildings in our backyard. Bible verses spoke to visitors from the sides of our buildings and on signs my father began

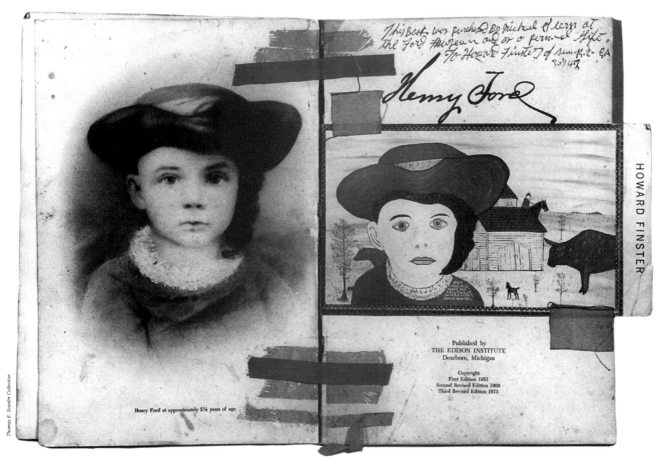

Thomas E. Scanlin Collection

Henry Ford at approximately 2½ years of age.

HOWARD FINSTER

Published by
THE EDISON INSTITUTE
Dearborn, Michigan

Copyright
First Edition 1953
Second Revised Edition 1960
Third Revised Edition 1973

My dad created this display using the first portrait he painted of Henry Ford, and the drawing from the book that inspired him.

posting along the shining pathways in our backyard. It seemed our backyard turned into a sacred gallery almost overnight. Among the buildings in our backyard, he started hanging his paintings at every turn. A walk through our backyard meant that you would come face to face with angels, Jesus, and serpents. There were pictures of presidents, Elvis, and great inventors such as Henry Ford. Even though my father didn't build any mansions in our backyard, he brought them back to life with his paintbrush. Soon, he was painting everything, turning ordinary things into extraordinary works of art. Coke bottles, jars, irons, and trash cans were transformed by my father's steady hand. I'm sure if I stood still long enough, my father would have painted me, too. To him, anything stationary was a painting waiting to happen.

It may come as a surprise to people familiar with my father's art, but he never intended to sell his work. Even though he was painting all his days

An old iron my father painted early in his artist career. I bought it from him in the mid-1970s.

A painted concrete sculpture of me at age nine.

and late into his nights, even though he began treating his painting as his new full-time job, my father didn't think his work was good enough to sell. Besides, he wasn't painting for profit or to call attention to himself. In his mind, his only mission was to bring new converts to God's altar by showing them glimpses of Heaven on canvas and Coke bottles. My father was simply advertising the word of God in our backyard for all the visitors who passed through our gate.

Living in a small town, word traveled quickly. Our backyard soon was crowded with new visitors who wanted to see what that Baptist minister was up to with all that paint. Even then, there were some people in town who turned up their noses. Not everyone in town was a critic, though. Some started asking him to bring his paint into their homes. He always agreed and never charged anyone a dime for his work. In fact, during his early painting years, he often gave his paintings away, hoping that his painted visions would open up a path in peoples' hearts big enough for God to walk through. Moved by my father's painted sermons, a woman from our old congregation at Chelsea

A sale sign Howard found and wrote on.

Baptist Church approached him one day and asked him if he would paint the headboard on her bed. I don't know what picture my father painted there, but I'd like to imagine she still sleeps with angels keeping watch over her head.

Back when my father was a preacher, he converted a lot of people to the Lord. With his gentle and unassuming way, he had managed to convert both Warner and Edith Wilson, along with their

Thomas E. Scanlin Collection

My father painted this depiction of Matthew: 7-22 in 1975 and nailed it to the outside of the Bible House.

MAT-7=22-MANY WILL SAY TO ME IN THAT DAY, LORD, HAVE WE NOT PROPHESIED IN THY NAME? AND IN THY NAME HAVE CAST OUT DEVILS? AND IN THY NAME DONE MANY WONDERFUL WORKS? AND THEN WILL I PROFESS UNTO THEM, I NEVER KNEW YOU: DEPART FROM ME, YE THAT WORK INIQUITY.

anyone who would listen long enough. My father has always been a humble man and was never one to advertise himself. So there is little doubt in my mind that if it had not been for Edith and all her phone calls, my father's art might never

children. And so when he began painting, Edith was quickly converted into one of his biggest fans. My father has always taught me that if you do a good turn for someone, if you treat people right, the favor comes back around eventually. He taught me that when the favor comes back around, it often returns to you tenfold. Well, that certainly was the case with Edith, because before my father caught on to what she was up to, Edith was busily calling art galleries far and wide, bragging about my father's work to

have traveled outside of our backyard.

Eventually, Edith's persistence found a willing ear in the Atlanta Council for the Arts. Soon after, the world became my father's church and his Bible verses and painted visions were sermonizing to crowds of people in art galleries all over the country. His art appeared in galleries throughout Atlanta; New York City; Chicago; Washington, D.C.; Louisiana; and Florida. Universities started calling, wanting my father to teach art classes. Reporters from television stations, magazines, and newspapers started showing up at my father's doorstep, wanting to interview this Baptist preacher who seemed to turn the art world upside down overnight. I think my father was stunned by all of the attention. After awhile, Paradise Garden was crawling with curiosity-seekers looking to buy up pieces of my father's art. One day, a woman from New York showed up in our backyard. My father didn't know at the time that she'd traveled all that way to see what all the fuss was about. Walking through our garden, she spotted a small painting of Noah's Ark, and she told my father she wanted to buy it. My father's first response was that it wasn't for sale, that it was painted for decoration in our garden. But this woman from New York was persistent, and my father finally agreed to sell her the painting for about twenty-five dollars. He did some other paintings for this woman, too. Shortly afterward, Paradise Garden was full of people just like that woman, wanting to buy any art my father was willing to part with. I remember one man even bought a trash can my father had painted and placed in our yard. In the early years of his art career, my father didn't put price tags on his works. Often when people offered to buy his paintings, he'd simply accept the amount they were willing to give in exchange. Money never did matter much to my father. As long as he had enough to live on and support his family, he was a happy man.

It was sometime after my father started painting that God came calling again. God made it clear to my father that he was to paint 5,000 pieces of art. So every time my father completed one of his paintings, he'd paint a number on it, sometimes along with the time of day he'd finished the work. On a piece of cardboard, my father started keeping a running tally of all the paintings he'd completed. It didn't take long for my father to surpass the 5,000 mark. Once he started painting, it seemed he required less and less sleep. He'd stay up half the night in his studio, painting his dreams and visions. Some nights he wouldn't crawl into bed until the sun came up and the birds started chirping. During those hours when the world was quiet and still asleep, my father was sometimes able to turn out as many as six paintings by the time the moon slipped below the horizon. I've always stood in awe of my

Dad painted the cover for his first book, published in 1982. The book is about his family and his preaching. He still sells these books for about five dollars apiece. The name of this self-published book is Vision of 200 Light Years Away Space Born of Three Generations From Earth to the Heaven of Heavens. *He wrote and illustrated the entire book after he started attracting attention from the art world.*

father, because he has this ability to paint for hours on end without stopping. The only explanation I can come up with is that God sits by my father all night long, and when my father's painting hand gets too tired to move, God takes over and finishes the job.

It has been many years since my father first painted the picture of George Washington from that dollar bill in 1976. And even though he's recognized the world over for his art, he is still the same humble man he's always been. My father doesn't take credit for his reputation as an artist. To Howard Finster, his paintbrush is just a conduit for God, and he just happens to be the medium through which God has chosen to speak. I am thankful that my father is now getting the recognition he's long deserved. But I'm also grateful I had all those years with him before I had to start sharing him with the rest of the world. Since my father's painting career took off, he's been on the move from one art gallery to the next, jet-setting all over the country. With the throngs of people who seem to gravitate toward my father, it's often been difficult to edge in time with him. In the past several years, though, he has started staying closer to home, similar to the tail end of his days as a traveling preacher. A short time ago, my father was one of seven artists chosen by several people in the art world to tour Europe. It was a great honor for my father, but he said his thank-yous and politely declined because he didn't want to leave my mother alone for all those weeks.

Even so, my father paints every chance he gets. At last count, he had completed painting number 46,902. Many of his paintings now sell for thousands of dollars, but I will never sell the ones hanging on my walls. One of my favorites is called "The Lord Will Deliver People Across Jordan." It's a picture of the Lord. In the picture, Jesus is gathering people to Him in the water, just like my father did all those years as a preacher when he was baptizing his converts. In his painting, beyond the riverside are tall mansions reaching up into a blue sky. When I look at that painting, I am reminded of all the mansions my father built us in Trion, now long gone. Sometimes if I stare at that painting long enough, a feeling of sadness washes over me.

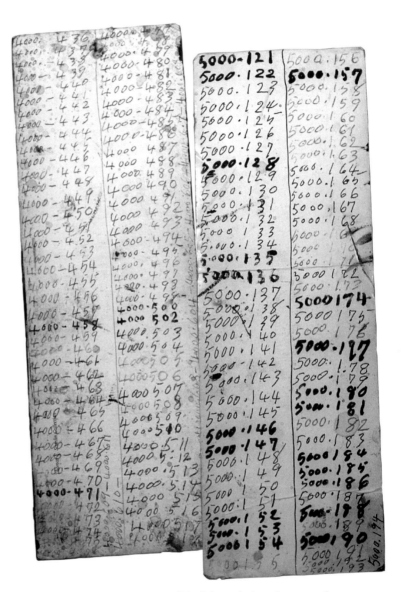

My father kept a running tally of the paintings he created. These pieces of cardboard document his accomplishment of painting five thousand—and beyond.

133

CHAPTER 10
MY GUARDIAN ANGEL WEARS PAINT-SPECKLED CLOTHES

Even though my father has kept our mansions alive in his paintings, the ones I grew up with in Trion are long gone.

Sometimes on the way to visit my parents, who now live in Summerville, I go down Highway 27 to gaze at the place where I grew up in Trion. Looking at what is left of the old house and now vacant backyard, it sometimes feels as though I'm trying to will the past back into existence. The front of the first story of the house my father built us still stands, but all his mansions and my old playhouse have vanished like the sand castles he built every year on the beaches in Florida. Sometimes I stop the car in front of the house. If I squint hard enough so that my vision blurs a little, I can almost imagine the rise of the miniature church steeple and the front porch of my playhouse. Every time I pull away from that house, I feel a little more of my past slipping between my fingers—as though I am trying to hold onto creek water. I cannot hope to hold onto a past that I cup like jewels in the palms of my hands. But fortunately during the baptism of my years, I have somehow managed to gather, collect, and preserve most memories of my childhood.

When I drive past the house and through the streets of Trion, it's easier for me to pretend everything has remained untouched by the passage of years. The normal progression of time and change seem to have bypassed the little mill town where I spent all those happy years. The name of the mill has long since changed, but many people who live in Trion still make their living inspecting cloth and sweeping floors in the mill, just like my father did so many years ago. The little mill houses still stand with their modest front porches and neatly manicured lawns. Somehow, it's a comfort to know that a handful of our old congregation at Chelsea Baptist Church,

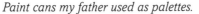

Paint cans my father used as palettes.

Thomas E. Scanlin Collection

135

including my best friend Reba, still walk through the doors of that sanctuary every Sunday. I know that if I were to show up one Sunday for a service, I'd see familiar faces sitting there in the pews.

As for our old backyard in Pennville, I haven't returned for several years. After we all married, moved off, and started our own families, my parents continued living in their house on the edge of Paradise Garden. But after my father's painting began attracting the attention of the art world and the national media, my parents no longer had privacy. Suddenly interested to see the place where my father's art began, people started showing up in droves. Eager to catch a glimpse of my father, they rang the doorbell and called

A stool Dad converted into a paint palette.

Thomas E. Scanlin Collection

on the phone at all hours. My parents have had a long series of unlisted phone numbers. Someone always manages to scout out their number, and soon their phone is back to ringing off the hook.

After several years of my father's fame and the resulting intrusion into their private lives, my parents were forced to make a difficult decision. They moved to a new home several miles away. Had it been entirely up to my father, I don't think he ever would have left the corner of paradise that he spent so many years building for us. But out of respect for my mother's need for privacy, he agreed to relocate to a more comfortable home in Summerville. After the move, my mother was finally able to walk out her back door without having to face flashes from tourists' cameras. My father returned to our garden every Sunday to meet all his visitors and deliver his impromptu sermons. When his health permits, he still returns there on Sundays.

Though he visits our backyard often, my father no longer owns Paradise Garden. Living several miles away, the garden became increasingly difficult to maintain. Several years ago, Beverly bought the garden from my father and the rest of the family. She does the best she can to keep up the buildings and the grounds, but I'm sure she agrees that no one has my father's touch. Without that touch, Paradise Garden seems to me like some sort of Eden that's slowly, sadly, and surely going the way of all our mansions in Trion.

The Bible House, which Dad covered with Bible verses, now belongs to a collector.

Many of the buildings in Paradise Garden have vanished or gradually surrendered to the elements. Visitors began offering to buy some of the buildings and attractions that had always been fixtures of my childhood. My father has never objected to sharing what he owned, and over time, when collectors and Finster fans began walking into his garden, he started selling some of those treasures. The Bible House is no longer in our garden. A collector from Atlanta bought that little house and hauled it away one sad afternoon.

Other landmarks that dotted the landscape of my youth have also disappeared from the park. Sections of the sidewalk my father painstakingly

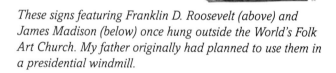

built over a period of years have also disappeared, bought up by collectors. Disappearing, too, are peoples' memories of what the park used to look like when it was still our little corner of paradise. Buildings that still stand in our garden are beginning to show their age, and some of the wooden structures are deteriorating into shells of their former glory. It is that process of decay that I can't bear to witness anymore. That's why I no longer return to our backyard in Pennville. When I reminisce about our yard, I'm not sure which is worse—trying to visualize the mansions that are only alive in my memory or having observed their decline.

These signs featuring Franklin D. Roosevelt (above) and James Madison (below) once hung outside the World's Folk Art Church. My father originally had planned to use them in a presidential windmill.

It's a shame to me that few people had the opportunity to experience Paradise Garden in its prime. I consider it even worse that some who had the chance to appreciate my father's early art squandered that opportunity because our backyard didn't fit their definition of normal. I remember when my father first began building our backyard park in Pennville and how some of our neighbors openly criticized some of the visions of paradise my father was trying to make real. I guess they didn't understand his visions or how he was trying to save the world from sin by painting Bible verses all over our buildings. I think most of those people misunderstood how he was trying to honor the genius of humankind by trying to collect everything ever invented by man. Back then, if you recycled people's throwaways and found a use for them, you weren't considered ingenious or friendly to the environment; instead, you were often considered more of a trash collector. I wasn't entirely oblivious to the criticism my father endured during those early years in Pennville, but I've always understood what he was trying to accomplish. We weren't the most popular kids in school, but even back then, what other people thought of my father didn't matter to me. I think some people in town probably thought him a little odd.

To me, he's always been the smartest, most inventive, most spiritual person in my world. And as I've gotten older, my admiration and appreciation for everything he taught me in church, in his workshop, and by example have steadily increased. As an adult, I fully appreciate the extent of his courage in the face of ridicule. No matter what people thought, he continued to build his dreams. Not only did he see Heaven in that backyard, but others eventually saw it, too.

It's funny how criticism stops when fame rings your doorbell or shadows your daily routine. When

(Above) This gourd, which depicts the cow jumping over the moon surrounded by spaceships, once hung in our garden.
(Below) Lyndon Johnson was once nailed to a post next to the small stream running through the garden.

139

The Sound of Howard Finster Man of Visions Worlds Minister of Folk Art Church, Inc.

(THE HUNTERS DREAM) OCT-28 1968

LATE IN THE EVENING. INTO THE NIGHT FALL. IN THE SHADOW OF THE MOON LIGHT THE WHIPPERWILL CALLS. INTO THE BIG TIMBER FAR INTO THE HILLS THE HUNTERS GUN IS LOADED TO KILL. HE CRUSHES ON THROUGH THE BROKEN LIMBS. HIS HOUNDS ARE HOT ON THE TRAIL.
I CAN HEAR HIM SAY OLD SPORT IS AHEAD I NEVER KNEW HIM TO FAIL. WHAT A BEAUTIFUL SOUND AS THE RACE GOES ON. THE RED FOX IS OUT TO NIGHT. THE JOY. AND SPORT. OF A HUNTERS LIFE. FOR THIS WAS HIS DELIGHT.
WHERE THE WISE OLD OWEL SOUNDS OFF HIS VOICE. THE ECHO COMES BACK TO ME. I KNOW THERES. TWO BIG ROUND BRIGHT EYES, SOME WHERE HIGH IN A TREE. ON DOWN THE WAY BY A LITTLE BROOK WITH HIS LIGHT ON A DRIFT OF SAND. FRESH COON TRACKS. MY WHAT A HUNTING LAND.
IS THIS A DREAM. ARE IS IT TRUE. I THINK IV. FOUND A DEER TRAIL TOO. ON THROUGH THE NIGHT TIME SWIFTLY PASSED. I SOON FOUND A LONG SMOOTH ROCK AT LAST. INTO MY SLEEPING BAG. I ZIPPED MY SELF AWAY.
I FELL ASLEEP LIKE LITTLE BOY BLUE. IN A BIG STACK OF HAY. THE MORNING SLIPPED UPON ME. THE SUN KISSED MY FACE. ALL FOUR OF MY OLD HOUND DOGS HAD JUST FINISHED THEIR RACE. THEY WERE LYING AROUND MY ROCKY BED TAKING A LITTLE NAP TOO. FAR AWAY IN THE BEAUTIFUL MOUNTAIN. WHERE THE SKYE IS HEAVENLY BLUE.
THE OLD WISE OWEL AND THE WHIPPERWILL WAS SILENT AS THE MORNING DEW. THE PEACE AND CALM OF THE WILDS LAY SO STILL. FROM THE HIGHEST MOUNTAIN TO THE LOWEST HILL. THE HUNTERS DREAM TO SHORT TO KNOW. LIKE A FEW MOMENTS OF A BIG RAINBOWE. LIKE MANNY COLORS OF ONE GREAT SIGHT. IT ONLY LASTED ONE SHORT NIGHT.

COMPOSED. OCT-28 1968
BY Howard Finster
Summerville R-#2
Georfie 30?4?
Phone 853-3436

My father composed this song, "Hunters Dream," on October 28, 1968.

Howard always loved music and recorded the Sound of Howard Finster, Man of Visions *in the early 1980s.*

my father finally gained the recognition he'd long deserved, the critics in town suddenly grew quiet. I guess the stream of reporters, collectors, and curiosity-seekers finally validated for them all the visions my father had long since validated for himself. Even though he believed in his artistic visions, I don't think he ever imagined that his art would be the topic of magazine articles, newspaper stories, and television shows. From the beginning, the only thing he hoped was that his sermons and visions in paint would reach all the people he had been unable to reach during his years as a traveling preacher. So when reporters from *People* magazine, *The Wall Street Journal*, *Esquire*, *Life* magazine, and the *Atlanta Journal-Constitution* began arriving at his doorstep for interviews, he was happier for the opportunity to spread his word to a wider audience than he was for all the attention bestowed on him. It was with that same spirit that he agreed to appear on the Johnny Carson show and paint album covers for R.E.M. and the Talking Heads.

Some artists spend their lives trying to paint their way into some of the New York City galleries that feature my father's work. But my father has never painted to further himself or his career. In fact, his success was really incidental. It was a byproduct of what he was aiming toward, which was to reach as many people as he could through his paintbrush. He's measured

My father was particularly proud of the award-winning cover for the Talking Heads' Little Creatures album because each of the many copies that sold contained thirty-five of his messages.

141

Thomas E. Scanlin Collection

My father used to host groups of schoolchildren at the World's Folk Art Church for what he called "art workouts."

his success not by the number of paintings he has sold or the number of galleries that have featured his art, but by the people he has reached through his painted visions. Through paint, Howard Finster has reached more people and turned more lives around than he did when he was preaching behind a pulpit.

Many people have bought his art for his painting talent alone. But he has always put a little bit of God in everything he's made, and that's how he's managed to spread the good news to so many people who otherwise would never have read passages from the Bible.

After word spread about my father's art, our town became a busier place. People started calling my father and officials in town to ask for directions to Paradise Garden. Eventually, the city posted signs on the main highways, pointing tourists in the right direction. It wasn't until my father became famous that the town even had a McDonald's. Over time, former critics had little to complain about and little else to say about our backyard park. In that way, my father really had the last laugh.

When confronted by angry townspeople, my father never said a harsh word back to them. Instead, he listened to what they had to say and quietly went about his business, continuing to build our backyard park. I learned from him that no one can take away your visions and dreams unless you let them. And I learned that if you allow someone to kill your dreams, you are allowing that person or those people to stamp out what's most important— God's plan for your life.

The current roadside sign in Pennville, Georgia.

Many people who achieve success, fame, and wealth forget the motivations that allowed those achievements to happen in the first place. Their priorities shift, and soon they are motivated only by more money, more success, and more fame. They buy bigger cars and bigger houses and lose their purpose in the process. My father is one of a rare breed who has remained virtually unchanged by all the temptations that success and fame can bring. The only thing that hasn't changed since his name

Dad's workspace in one of the houses he owned in Pennville.

became associated with the art world is my father himself. He's still the same man today as he was during my childhood. He is still the same preacher, the same father who worked hard all the days of his life so his family could afford the luxuries he couldn't when he was growing up in Alabama. Even with more money than he ever dreamed of earning, he lives far below his means.

My parents still live in the house they bought eleven years ago in Summerville. My father still buys used cars just as he did before he became famous. He still saves everything, including every pen he's ever used, whether it works or not. When a coffee can is emptied, he saves it for future use. My father still prefers to eat his banana pudding before dinner and still wears the same paint-speckled clothes he wore when he first started painting.

About the only evidence that my parents have stumbled into more money than they used to have is my father's insistence on buying my mother a new Lincoln every few years to make sure she has a safe ride while running her errands. And sometimes when he walks into art-supply stores, he drops three to four hundred dollars at a time on paint and other

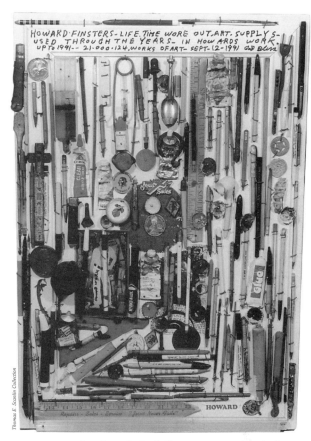

Thomas E. Scanlin Collection

Just a sample of my father's "wore out art supplys" from doing more than 46,000 works of art. In the center of this piece, number 21,124, is a cross bearing the message, "Jesus Saves."

supplies. In recent years, when Dad has bought new clothes and shoes, they always stay clean but most of them are spattered with paint. When you meet Howard Finster, you're meeting a real person, a true artist who has remained untouched by fame and

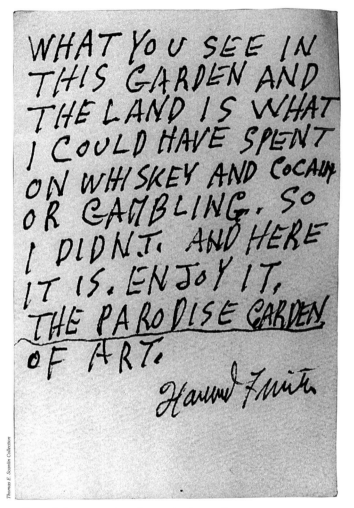

WHAT YOU SEE IN THIS GARDEN AND THE LAND IS WHAT I COULD HAVE SPENT ON WHISKEY AND COCAIN OR GAMBLING. SO I DIDN.T. AND HERE IT IS. ENJOY IT, THE PARODISE GARDEN OF ART.

Howard Finster

Thomas E. Scanlin Collection

One of the many thought cards Howard Finster created during his life.

fortune. He knows everything good in his life has resulted from hard work and God meeting him more than halfway.

In my world, my father is one person who has always had his priorities straight. Even after fame and fortune catapulted him into the spotlight, he has remained a humble man. For that alone, I am most proud to claim Howard Finster as my father.

He still paints every day he can, often driven to exhaustion by his need to spread the message of God. Sometimes he paints late into the night, fired by visions of Heaven and words God is telling him to commit to canvas. He has always felt that saving souls was a race against time, a race against all the visions and predictions revealed in Revelations.

Lately he has spent an increasing amount of time shuttling between his home and doctors' offices. The times I've driven him to the doctor, he has always carried his paint pens and a couple of pieces of art to work on. When I glance over at him in the passenger seat, I often see him painting his visions of Heaven. I see a man trying to beat time with his paintbrush.

As I write, my father approaches age 86. He has become more forgetful than he used to be. Several months ago, he flew to New York for an art show. He returned from his tour with a bad case of pneumonia. One problem led to another, and a couple of months after his return, a blood clot migrated to one of his lungs. Confined to bed during his recovery, he was unable to paint and unable to focus on anything except survival.

Sitting at his bedside and watching him sleep during those long days and nights, I realized he wasn't too worried about dying. He's seen glimpses of Heaven all his life and knows the peace that awaits him on the other side. I realized that, more than dying, my father fears leaving his family behind. And he fears running out of time before he finishes painting the sermons and visions God has fed to him every day of his life.

One night during his illness, the sudden movement of his hand startled me. Although he had been unable to paint for days, my father's painting hand shot up into the air while he slept. I watched in silent fascination as his fingers began working a paintbrush against a canvas only visible to him in his dream. For the next few minutes, he continued painting this invisible picture several inches above his bed. I couldn't see the colors of his imagination or the shapes pouring out onto his canvas. Still I

Howard busy creating another piece of art in the garden.

knew he was outlining the forms of angels and painting his corner of Heaven.

I consider myself blessed to see my father's visions take shape in his art once again. The illness unsettled me, and since his recovery I have found my mind returning to a conversation my father and I had years ago while walking one evening across a bridge in our backyard in Pennville. I was about twenty-five at the time, and my two children were off playing in some other corner of the garden. As we crossed the bridge, taking in the peace of the trickling creek and the scent of nearby flowers, he suddenly broke the silence. My father has always had an uncanny knack for reading my mind. Prior to our walk, I had been worrying about how hard he was working in the garden, fearing that he was hammering his way to a heart attack. As we walked on the bridge, he stopped, turned to me, and said, "I don't want you grieving over me or worrying about when I die. When that day comes, I want you to be happy for me because I'll be headed to a place where there won't be any sadness or sorrow."

I don't remember whether I said anything in response, but my father's brief statement did nothing to calm my mind at the time. It made me wonder whether he was keeping something from me, whether he really was dying. Then I slowly came to realize that he was simply trying to reassure me about death, that the end of life is nothing to fear if you are right with the Lord. In recent years I've come to realize the wisdom of those words. Even so, I dread the day when I'll have to call on that wisdom.

I know that one day I won't be able to walk the full length of that bridge with my father anymore. I know that I can't hope to hold onto him forever. He was never mine to keep in the first place. I know that our loved ones are only on loan to us for a short time and that God eventually calls them all back home. As my father's daughter, I've always known that God sometimes sends angels to earth in human form. My guardian angel has always been a man of visions who wears paint-speckled clothes. He has devoted his life to saving souls, sharing everything he knows of Heaven. On the day my father is called to God's altar, I will know with certainty that he'll walk down a shining, jeweled path toward a city of mansions glittering in gold.

(TRUE EXPERENCE)

i STOPPED BY THE SIDE OF THE ROAD ONE DAY. i BOUGHT A
TRACK OF LAND. i FILLED THE DITCHES, AND SMOOTHED THE MOUNDS
WITH MY OWN TWO WORKING HANDS.
IN THE HEART OF PENNVILLE i CLEARED AWAY A JUNGLE SLIGHTLY
CLEAN. i OPENED UP ~~THE~~ A CHANNEL FOR THREE CLEAR WATER
STREAMES, i FENCED IT IN, DUG LILLY PONDS, FOR FISH AND OTHER
THING, INCLUDING A HOUSE WITH SEVEN ROOMS WHERE THE BEAUTIFUL
BIRDS SING, i PLANTED VINES, AND TREES, AND A VECETABLE
GARDEN THAT GROWS, i GIVE A SAMPLE OF THE FRUIT TO PEOPLE
WHO COMES AND GOES, WITH A FLOCK OF GEESE TO PICK THE
GRASS. PEACOCKS TO BEAUTIFY THE PEN. AND DUCKS TO SWIM
THE WATERS AND THE LITTLE BANTAM HENS, i BUILT A
CRAFTMANS WOOD SHOP AND MAKE THE STRANGEST THINGS
AROUND, WHILE MY HENS LAY EGGS ON MY WORK BENCH AND
SOME TIMES ON THE GROUND, i COMPOSED ABOUT ONE THOUSAND
ARTICLES, WITH REACORDS AND SONG OF MY OWN, i HAVE A ELECTRIC
GETTIBE SOME TIMES i PLAY A SONG, i BUILT A SHOE OF CONCRET-
IT WILL WEIGH ABOUT A TON AND A HALF i DISPLAYED ABOUT ONE
THOUSAND COLLECTIONS FOR PEOPLE WHO COME. AND PASS.
ROSES THAT BLOOM BY THOUSAND. FLOWERS OF DIFFEREN KINDS,
WITH BIRD BOXES BIRDS. AND PEGIONS AMONG THE TREES AND
EVEN GOARD VINES. i DO MY OWN PLMING, AND WIRING MY CARPENTING
AND MASON WORK. DO MY OWN BOOKS OF RECORDS I AM THE
SECUTARY AND CLERK. MY SHORTEST STOCK ON HAND. IS TIME.
THAT i DO NOT WASTE. EVEN ON MY WOODWORK A LITTLE MESSAGE i
PASTE. ALL THESE THINGS ARE AS VAPOUR TO VANISH AND PASS AWAY
THE ONLY TRUE JOY i KNOW IS TO SERVE THE LORD EVERY DAY
        COMPOSED 1:25 RM: aug 2-1970
        BY HOWARD FINSTER
        SUM BA GA- 30748
        Ph. 857 29-26

149

HOLY *IS A* MIND, DRIFT, INTO TIME, KEEPS ME IN LINE, SO I FEEL FINE. AND WALK IN LINE LONG THE RIVERS. OF SHRINE. ITS PEACIFUEL. TO MY MIND. WHY CANT IT HAPPEN ALL THE TIME I ASK YOU. TO STAY IN LINE. MAKE IT TO HEAVEN. ALL A WINNER OF ALL TIME I. DEDICATE POEM TO T. J. BRADSHAW". this

composed @ 5:45 A.m.
May 23rd 2001
Howard Finster

To Thelma, Thanks to you and G.C. For all your help over the years.
May God Bless and keep you
Love Mother

Thomas E. Scanlin Collection

Howard and Pauline Finster wrote this message of thanks to Thelma for her work on this book.

Holy is a mind,
Drift into time,
Keeps me in line,
So I feel fine,
and walk in line,
long the rivers of shrine
its peacifuel to my mind
why can't it happen all the time
I ask you to stay in line,
make it to heaven,
a winner of all time.

—Howard Finster

Pauline and Howard in recent years.

ACKNOWLEDGMENTS

First I would like to thank John Denton—without him this book would not have happened. I met John in the early 1980s in Dad's park. When he found out I was Howard Finster's daughter, we struck up a conversation that lasted an hour or more. After that we kept running into each other either at the park or an art show. Somehow we would always end up having long conversations about my dad and my growing up years. Every now and then John would say, "You need to write a book." Eventually he suggested we make a videotape so that he could find a publisher for my story. John went to considerable trouble to make that tape, and soon my book was in the making. So John I give you most of the credit for this book. Thank you so much!

Jenny Cromie, thank you for all those hours you spent on the phone with me, listening to my stories. You are the greatest, and I feel like I got to know you very well. It was you who helped me turn all those stories into a book.

Thanks to all my church family, especially Mozell and J.H. Willingham, Edith and Warner Wilson, Reba Garner Gill, and also in loving memory of Shirley Willingham McCrickard, one of my best friends. Thank you all for sharing pictures and stories with me.

Thomas Scanlin, you and I have one thing in common— the love we have for my parents. You care for them so much; you could almost be one of their children. More than once you and I have visited into the late-night hours, sharing stories about our respective times with Mom and Dad. They love all your visits and the things you do for them, especially the trips you take them on. My mother still talks about the picnic, and Snoopy riding in your Rolls Royce. Thank you for caring, and thank you for your interest and encouragement regarding my book. The many hours you spent going through pictures, organizing, and providing materials have been invaluable. I know you have a special place in the hearts of my parents. I wish you the best with your folk art museum.

Thank you also to a long-time friend of the family, Victor Faccinto, for contributing some of your photographs to the book.

A special thanks to my husband G.C. Bradshaw and my children Stephanie, Jon, Paul, and Eli for being so patient with me in getting my book together. Thank you for your help and encouragement.

Thank you Mom and Dad for going back to the early years to recall stories, dates, and places for me. You are the greatest.

Shelley DeLuca, thank you for all the help in finalizing my book. You have a lot of patience in working with people. That makes you very special.

Most of all, thank you to Ellen Sullivan and Crane Hill Publishers for wanting to publish this book of memories that means so much to me.